# ITALY

### THE VEGETARIAN TABLE

# ITALY
## THE VEGETARIAN TABLE

BY JULIA DELLA CROCE

PHOTOGRAPHY BY DEBORAH JONES

FOOD STYLING BY SANDRA COOK

WITH LOCATION PHOTOGRAPHY BY ALAN BLAUSTEIN

CHRONICLE BOOKS · SAN FRANCISCO

# DEDICATION

❀

To my mother, Giustina Ghisu della Croce, from whom I learned that eating is holy.
And to my children, Gabriella Leah and Celina Raffaella, in hopes that someday they will eat vegetables.

Text and recipes copyright © 1994 by Julia della Croce.
Food photographs copyright © 1994 by Deborah Jones.
Location photographs copyright © 1994 by Alan Blaustein.
All rights reserved. No part of this book may be reproduced in any form without
written permission from the publisher.

Library of Congress Cataloging-in-Publication Data:
Della Croce, Julia
The vegetarian table: Italy/by Julia della Croce; photography by Deborah Jones.
p. cm
Includes index.
ISBN 0-8118-0458-5
1. Vegetarian cookery. 2. Cookery, Italian. I. Title
TX837.D35 1994
641.5′636′0945—dc20                    94-870
CIP

Editing: Sharon Silva
Book and Jacket Design: Louise Fili Ltd.
Design Assistant: Leah Lococo
Photo Styling: Sara Slavin

Printed in Hong Kong

Distributed in Canada by Raincoast Books,
112 East Third Avenue, Vancouver, B.C. V5T 1C8

10 9 8 7 6 5 4 3 2 1

Chronicle Books
275 Fifth Street
San Francisco, CA 94103

# CONTENTS

✦

# ACKNOWLEDGMENTS

❀

**M**Y GREATEST THANKS GO TO MY MOTHER, GIUSTINA GHISU DELLA CROCE, FROM WHOM I LEARNED AT AN EARLY AGE TO HONOR THE LIVING THINGS WHOSE LIVES ARE SACRIFICED TO SUSTAIN OUR OWN. And I thank my father, Giovanni della Croce, for infecting me with his passion for the vegetable garden even before I cut my first teeth. For help with my researches, I thank my sister Justine and her husband, Charles Kadoche. I also thank my aunt Rita Ghisu for her painstaking translations of Sicilian sources; my network of family in Sardinia and Rome—especially my cousins Agnese Basieu, Ida Basieu Falconi, and Zaira Piga Savonna—whose efforts to help me research the Sardinian table included personal deliveries of *carta di musica* ("music paper bread") smuggled from Cagliari to my New York City kitchen; and my aunts Anna and Nella Ghisu, who have not only helped with my researches about Sardinian food, but whose impeccable and beguiling cooking has been an inspiration for my books. I am grateful to Gisella Isidori and to Giuseppe Grappolini for adding to my knowledge of olive oil, and to Gisella and her husband, Cristiano Isidori, for sharing their recipes; to Anna Amendolara Nurse for her generous recipe contributions; to Nick Malgieri for his advice on Italian baking; to the Honorable Boris Biancheri, Ambassador of Italy to the United States, for his assistance with recipes from his native Liguria; to Anna Guaita and Stefano Trincia for access to the work of their grandfather, the Duke of Salaparuta, whose book, *Cucina vegetariana e naturismo crudo*, provided historical and culinary insights into vegetarian eating in Sicily; to Dahlia Carmel, that indefatigable culinary sleuth, for sussing out hard-to-find sources on vegetarian literature; to Jean Amin, my extraordinary housekeeper, for her no-nonsense approach with a paring knife, and for her persistence with peppers in particular; to my friend, Flavia Destefanis, who devoted many hours to proofreading my manuscript; and to my assistant and friend, Peter Susser, without whose help—in the kitchen and out—this book could never have been completed on time. I am, as always, thankful to Nancy Q. Keefe, my *angelo custode*, to my agent, Judith Weber, for her guidance and unswerving professionalism, to my editor at Chronicle Books, Bill LeBlond, for giving me the opportunity to produce beautiful books, to Leslie Jonath for gently leading me through the editorial process, and to Sharon Silva for the extraordinary skill with which she transforms a manuscript into a book. I also thank the other individuals and restaurants who graciously contributed recipes to this book, or whose ideas have influenced me in some way. Deborah Jones wishes to thank Sara Slavin, prop stylist; Jeri Jones, photo assistant; Allyson Levy, food stylist assistant; Missy Hamilton and Roberto Varriale for their talented backgrounds, as well as Biordi Italian Imports, Fillamento, and Vivande for the generous use of their props.

# INTRODUCTION

❀

**I**N 1614, GIACOMO CASTELVETRO, AN EMILIAN NOBLEMAN EXILED IN ENGLAND, WROTE **A BRIEF ACCOUNT OF THE FRUITS, HERBS & VEGETABLES OF ITALY**. The guide was written with the intent to influence the British to introduce a greater quantity and variety of fruits and vegetables into their meat-based diet. In the opening chapter, he wrote,

> "I often reflect upon the variety of good things to eat which have been introduced into this noble country of ours over the past fifty years. The vast influx of refugees from the evils and cruelties of the Roman Inquisition has led to the introduction of delights previously considered inedible, worthless or even poisonous. Yet I am amazed that so few of these delicious and health-giving plants are being grown to be eaten. Through ignorance or indifference, it seems to me that they are cultivated less for the table than for show by those who want to boast of their exotic plants and well-stocked gardens. This moves me to write down all I can remember of the names of the herbs, fruits and plants we eat in Italy, my civilized homeland, and to explain how to prepare them, either raw or cooked, for the table, so that the English no longer need be deprived through lack of information of the delights of growing and eating them. . . ."

It is ironic that Castelvetro's observations about English eating habits—which so influenced our own—are still applicable today. Certainly, America has a great abundance of vegetables. But the abundance is in terms of crop yields and plant size. For the most part, we too have relegated vegetables to side-dish status.

Written close to four hundred years ago, Castelvetro's message, to curtail consumption of meats, sweets, and overly rich dishes in the interests of health and good taste, is a timeless testimony to the wisdom of Italian cooking technique. He advises to live close to nature and to cook close to nature; that none but the simplest treatment of vegetables will result in retaining their full natural flavor; and that in the vegetable kingdom we will find our greatest source of nourishment and food for well-being.

The growing and cooking of vegetables has been a highly evolved aspect of the Italian kitchen since ancient times. Ironically, it was the Romans who laid much of the groundwork for the Italian passion for vegetables. Despite their militaristic proclivities, they ate little meat. The daily diet of the wealthy was comprised principally of bread, eggs, olives, cheese, and various vegetables. Meat and fish were eaten, but not every day. The poor ate porridges made from millet and various grains; a primitive, coarse bread; cheese; and a limited variety of fruits and vegetables. Cattle were raised principally for milk and cheese, not for meat. The Romans were highly skilled agriculturalists. Indeed, they were the first to write books on the subject. Virgil, Ovid, and Horace were among those whose important works reflected a deep knowledge of agronomy and botany. The expertise of the Italian farmer is due in no small part to the know-how of his ancient ancestors.

The Italian love of vegetables has continued until modern times. In a country where meat eating has been a privilege reserved for few until recent decades, grains, eggs, cheese, and vegetables have formed the foundation of the diet for the majority of the population. The reasons for this are not only historical and economic, but also geographical and religious.

At the very roots of the high quality of Italian vegetables are the temperate climate, long growing seasons, and hospitable landscape of the country, which combine to form the ideal environment for growing grains, vegetables, and fruits.

An equally important influence on the eating habits of Italians has been the dietary restrictions placed on the population by the Catholic church. For sixteen centuries, papal laws imposed strict dietary rules that forbade meat consumption during numerous holy days that amounted to one third of the days of the year. The *cucina di magro* (literally, "lean kitchen"), the fast-day kitchen, rejected all meats but allowed fish, dairy products, and all vegetables.

Thus, it is not surprising that while there has never been any real vegetarian movement in Italy, the Italian way with food has a vegetarian focus. Almost every course—the *antipasto*, the *primo* (first course), and the *contorno* (vegetable dish "surrounding" the second course)—is focused on vegetables and grains. The *secondo* (second course) is the traditional meat or fish course, but substantial baked pasta dishes, *polenta*, and bean dishes have also typically been second-course fare. And except on Sundays and holidays, the last course consists of fruit, which might be served raw, baked, poached, or grilled.

When I was growing up, I was surrounded by this love of vegetables that is so intrinsically Italian. One of my first memories of my mother is of her wading in a local stream, her wide cotton skirt of 1950s fashion lifted above her knees and tied in a knot as she foraged for watercress among the smooth rocks of the shallows. And I always remember my father sprawled in the grass on the wide lawn that surrounded our house, plucking and eating the tender leaves of the wild dandelions near where he lay.

Before we moved into that big house with its vast lawn and lots of room for a vegetable garden, we lived in an apartment house in Pearl River, a sleepy little hamlet on the New York–New Jersey border. My parents convinced the landlord to let them grow a garden on a small empty lot next to the community garage. There we planted tomatoes and cucumbers, among other things. I remember with perfect clarity my forays into that little plot that they struggled to win from the groundhogs and rabbits that raided it. My earliest memory of a tomato is the ambrosial snap as I plucked it from the vine, then the thrill of the first sweet, dusty bite. And the cucumbers! What a delight to pick the young ones off the vine and eat them while they were still dewy, crisp, and cool inside, the heat of the late summer sun still upon their tender skin.

But the sweetest memory I have is of the little fig trees that my grandfather, an Italian immigrant, nurtured in his backyard, in what is today the South Bronx. In 1908, when my grandparents bought the old brick house, it was surrounded by trees and by fields where the horses they kept to pull their ice wagon grazed. One of the first things my grandfather did was to plant a fig tree in his backyard. It was started from a twig that had made its way from the old country to the new, and from it he begot a whole generation. I remember grandpa's fig trees. They huddled against the high iron fence that was put up to protect the little house that remained in the neighborhood even after it became a notorious ghetto. When my grandmother died and the house was sold, my mother cut a little branch from one of those fig trees and planted it on the grounds of our house. It never bore the sweet, luscious figs it would have under the hot Mediterranean sun of her and my grandfather's native Italy, but we still relished the figs it produced every summer.

My grandfather was not the only Italian immigrant to transplant the flora of his homeland here. The Italian immigrants exported their know-how in growing food wherever they went. Italian settlers in California put in acres and acres of artichokes—for them a commonplace vegetable—and the state now produces over 70 million pounds a year. Other transplanted *contadini*—"farmers"—also began some of the country's greatest vineyards. They grew olives, herbs, eggplants, broccoli, and broccoli *rape*, and reintroduced the tomato, peppers, and other vegetables of their cherished cuisine.

In America today, the vegetables the Italians long ago tended have become not only familiar, but fashionable. But there are ethical, ecological, and medical considerations that make the case for greater vegetable consumption a compelling one. Scientific studies link excessive consumption of red meat to breast, colon, and prostate cancer, heart disease, atherosclerosis, and many other diseases of our time. Studies have shown that peoples who practice largely vegetarian diets outlive those who make meat a mainstay of their eating habits. The evidence seems irrefutable that a reduced-flesh diet leads to greater health, endurance, and longevity.

Some of the recipes in this book contain eggs, milk, cheese, and other dairy products. These meat products are not part of the diets of vegetarians who adhere strictly to regimens that eschew meat products. There are, however, many nonegg and nondairy recipes in these pages to satisfy vegetarians who avoid such foods.

For those who are concerned with the health aspect of eggs, I point out that while eggs are high in cholesterol, their protein content is also the highest of any food. Dairy products also contain cholesterol, but they are sources of protein as well. I believe that it is important to include these natural products in moderation. On the other hand, we should be vigilant in eschewing foods grown with or contaminated by toxins, or stripped of their natural goodness through improper or lengthy storage and handling.

The Italian way of eating is rich in its bounty of meatless choices. For the vegetarian, Italian markets, teeming with their lush displays of vegetables and fruits in dazzling colors, tended by jealous vendors guarding every treasure from the rude pinches of lusty customers, are temples. Even the dry-goods store is full of staples that are a vegetarian's delight: *polenta*, buckwheat, barley, wholesome rices, pungent dried *porcini* mushrooms, and the like.

Like Castelvetro, I am moved to write down all that I know of the delicious and health-giving way with vegetables that I was nourished on. I hope that this book will move readers to reproduce the variety and goodness of the Italian vegetarian table in American kitchens. One need not even be a vegetarian to enjoy the dishes in these pages. There are no taste compromises or calls for substitute foods developed to placate the taste for meat. The *cucina povera*, "poor kitchen," as the Italians affectionately call their peasant-influenced, vegetarian-based cuisine, is rich indeed in quality and flavor.

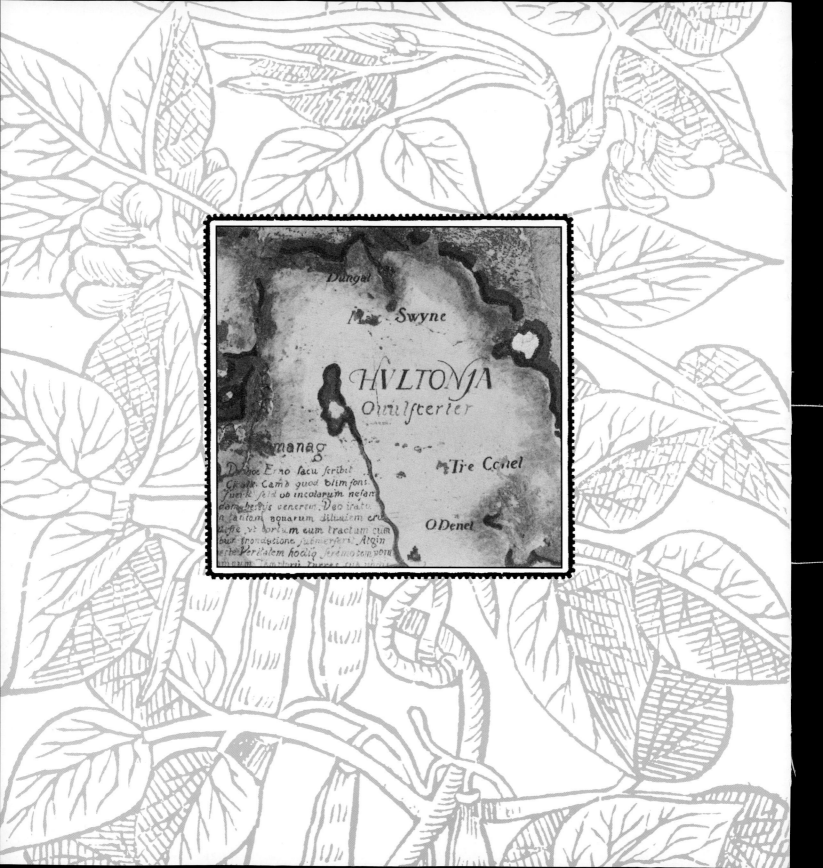

chapter one

FONDA-
MENTALI

fundamentals

TRUE ITALIAN COOKING CANNOT BE ACCOMPLISHED WITHOUT AN UNDERSTANDING OF THE BASIC INGREDIENTS AND THE DISTINCTLY ITALIAN APPROACH TO PUTTING THEM TOGETHER. In order to duplicate the unforgettable flavors of this extraordinary cuisine, one must be as familiar with its components as a composer is with the elements of music. The two things essential in reproducing authentic Italian vegetable and vegetarian dishes outside of Italy are, first, obtaining the freshest possible produce, and then, whenever possible, using genuine products such as imported Italian olive oil, olives, cheeses, and so on.

The Italian style of cooking is simple. There are few sauces, and certainly no elaborate ones that require lengthy preparation, reductions, clarifying, or what have you. But simplicity and a direct approach in employing ingredients is in contrast to lavish use of raw materials. As Elizabeth David writes in her classic volume, *Italian Food*, a work that single-handedly opened the eyes of postwar Britain to the glories of authentic Italian cooking, "The Italians, unlike the thrifty French, are very extravagant with raw materials. . . . [They] are used not so much with reckless abandon as with a precise awareness of what good quality does for the cooking." This "extravagance" is particularly important when it comes to vegetable cookery, for most vegetable dishes are quite elementary. If the few basic ingredients are not impeccable, there are no other ingredients to act as foils or to compensate for flavor that is lacking.

Take, for example, the call for ingredients in a recently published Sardinian cookbook, sent to me by a cousin in Cagliari. Recipes list such ingredients as "four eggs, just laid," "1 kilo of young, tender fava beans that have just been picked," "500 grams of the purest cream available," "1 medium-sized, tenderest possible cauliflower," "about 1 kilogram of sweet water eel, preferably the white autumnal variety that descend from the rivers toward the sea after the first rains," "a suckling pig bred from a pig that grazes from pasturage where there are oak trees and wild aromatic herbs," and so on.

While such descriptions might seem fantastical to the American reader, to the Italian, they are not. In Italy, one still hears such reveries and exhortations about food wherever one goes. From the taxi driver to the local priest, from the shopkeeper to the politician, food is everybody's business. I have gotten passionate advice on the only way to make a proper *pesto alla genovese* from a Roman luggage merchant. Once in Siena, after an exquisite meal of fresh *porcini*, I was driven by my waiter to the nearby Tuscan countryside to hunt for the wild mushrooms. I have received guidance on growing grapes, harvesting and pickling capers, and making homemade walnut liqueur by an Italian graduate student whom I hired to help me polish my Italian.

Certainly, my childhood is full of memories of this love of good food. It is spoken about with no less passion than *la guerra*, politics, or family. I am reminded of a conversation I had with my *zia* Nella, whom I called recently about an unforgettable vegetable soup (page 59) she cooked for us once when we visited her in Rome. After some talk about the soup, she complained bitterly about the state of things in Cerveteri, in the suburbs of Rome, where she now lives. "It's a *schifezza* [an untranslatable Italian word connoting a highly disgusting and loathsome situation]," she said, referring to the quality of the *parmigiano* cheese the local markets offered in her town. Rather than discuss the collapse of the Italian government, which had just occurred that day, she elaborated on her disgust at this state of gastronomical affairs by implicating the government and local producers in a conspiracy to pass off compressed, fermented mashed potatoes as *parmigiano-reggiano*. Her vituperations ended with threats to leave this sorry state of affairs and move elsewhere, perhaps to her native Sardinia.

Short of moving to a farm in the Italian countryside, eating only food that has just been harvested, or seeking out cheeses and such produced by skillful local artisans whose craft is a product of personal pride and centuries of know-how and tradition, how does an American experience this genuineness that makes real Italian cooking so very good? We are so used to eating food that doesn't taste of itself, that words alone are not sufficient to describe to the uninitiated the pleasure of green beans that are cooked minutes after they are picked, of dripping fresh, creamy mozzarella still warm from the cheesemaker's kettle, or of the flavor of just-pressed olive oil drizzled over a slab of fresh country bread that was lightly toasted over a wood fire. We are accustomed to vegetables that get to us weeks and even months after they are picked, so that what flavor they contain is a mere hint of what it should be.

But it is not an impossible task to obtain fresh and genuine ingredients. In the summer and fall, superb local farm-raised organic vegetables and fruits are sold in farmer's markets everywhere. And while it is true that the flavor and goodness of our vegetables suffer from modern methods of agriculture and from the problems of transporting food, fresh vegetables can be found in our supermarkets if one knows what to look for. Today, all the essential ingredients of the Italian pantry are imported, including cheeses, oils, vinegars, canned tomatoes, and so on. People who live in rural areas where these specialty foods are still hard to find can buy all of them, including cheeses, through the mail (see pages 158–159). We have only to insist on fresh and genuine ingredients and then apply the principles of simplicity of preparation and harmony of flavors.

BUTTER VERSUS OLIVE OIL

At the foundation of Italian cuisine are butter, olive oil, and, to a lesser extent today, lard. If an imaginary dividing line could be drawn across the Italian peninsula, it would show that the south of Italy, including its islands of Sicily and Sardinia, rely on the use of olive oil; northern cooks, in contrast, depend upon butter. This is not to say that butter is never used in the south, nor that olive oil is absent from the northern pantry. Indeed, many of Italy's great olive oils are produced in the central and northwestern regions of Tuscany and Liguria. But because the arid southern landscape does not support cattle, the foundation of cooking has been the oil of the tenacious olive tree. The southern regions have always been poorer and less developed than those of the north, an historical factor that has influenced bold, rustic local cuisines based on inexpensive, primarily nonmeat ingredients. The climate and geography of the verdant northern regions, on the other hand, have been conducive to the production of cattle and, therefore, butter. This fact on the one hand, and the gastronomical influences of France, Switzerland, and Austria on Italy's northern borders on the other, have established a butter-based cuisine in the north.

While the olive oil–based Mediterranean diet has become the focus of an America obsessed with cholesterol and calories, the importance of butter in Italian cooking should not be underestimated. It should be noted that only unsalted butter (also called sweet butter) is recommended. The flavor of unsalted butter is more delicate than that of salted butter; its clear, unmatchable sweetness is uncompromised by the imposing presence of salt. Unsalted butter is also more perishable, and it quickly absorbs the odors of foods to which it is exposed, so it is important to keep it covered and always refrigerated when not in use. For maximum freshness, store reserves of unsalted butter in the freezer rather than in the refrigerator. Fruity olive oil can be substituted for butter in many recipes, but certain dishes require the delicacy, sweeter flavor, and greater body that butter gives. *Risotti* would certainly fall into this category, as would certain vegetable side dishes.

This endorsement of unsalted butter is in no way intended to belittle the virtues of extra-virgin olive oil. Its heady aroma and fruity flavor is the soul of much of Italy's marvelous rustic and robust cooking. Put simply, true Italian cooking couldn't exist without it.

STAPLES

In addition to olive oil or butter, the staples of vegetarian cooking are eggs, cheese, beans, *polenta* (cornmeal), rice, pasta, capers, olives, and a few herbs and spices. Also, since meat is absent, a flavorful vegetable broth such as the excellent one in chapter 3 is useful to have on hand, particularly for soups, *risotti*, and *zuppa gallurese*, the lovely, savory Sardinian bread pudding in chapter 3. It is wise to make this broth in advance and keep it refrigerated or frozen so that the preparation of other dishes is simplified.

BEANS, IN ITALIAN, **FAGIOLI**. Shell beans, that is, fresh beans (not to be confused with green beans), are not commonplace in American markets. Such beans are commonly found dried here, but from time to time they are seen fresh, particularly cranberry beans and fava beans. Shell beans must be removed from their pods and the pods discarded. To cook, drop them in boiling water and simmer until they are tender. This will take a fraction of the cooking time required for dried beans.

Dried beans and lentils, however, are excellent. Rehydrating dried beans takes more time than opening a can, but I feel that the resulting firm texture of the beans makes the preparation worthwhile. An exception is dried chick-peas, which can be so hard that no manner of soaking and boiling will tenderize them. In any case, canned chick-peas remain firmer than other kinds of canned beans, so do not hesitate to substitute them for cooked dried chick-peas.

Other canned beans can be used in a pinch; just remember that their texture is very soft, so if they are cooked too long, they will fall apart. For bean salads, rinse canned beans with cold water and drain them thoroughly before dressing them. In recipes where beans are cooked with other ingredients, add canned beans for the last ten minutes of cooking and reduce the salt in the recipe to compensate for the canned beans' higher salt content.

Dried beans can become excessively hard if they have been stored for too long. Even lengthy presoaking will not rehydrate them sufficiently. If their skin is wrinkled, it is a sign they are too hard. It is wise to use dried beans within a year of purchase.

To rehydrate beans, first pick them over and discard any stones or any beans that are discolored or damaged. Put them in a large bowl and add cold water to cover by three inches. Let them stand at room temperature for a minimum of four hours, or for as long as overnight. Drain them and they are ready to be cooked. An alternative method is to put them in a large saucepan, add water to cover by three inches, and bring them to a boil. When the water boils, cover the pan and remove it from the heat. Let the beans stand for one hour, then drain and proceed with the cooking.

To cook rehydrated beans, put them in a pot with fresh water to cover by three inches. Bring to a boil and immediately reduce the heat to a simmer. Cover partially and cook gently until the beans are tender but not falling apart, about one hour.

Salt the beans only after cooking, or they will toughen. To store, transfer the beans and enough of their cooking liquid to cover the beans to a bowl or storage container; they can be refrigerated for up to five days, or frozen for up to three months.

BREAD CRUMBS, IN ITALIAN, **PANE GRATTUGIATO, PANE GRATTATO, OR PANGRATTATO.** Dried bread crumbs are used to thicken sauces, to coat sautéed and deep-fried foods, and to top baked dishes to form a crisp crust. They are also sprinkled onto greased pan surfaces to prevent baked dishes from sticking.

So-called flavored bread crumbs, also called Italian bread crumbs, often contain dried parsley and other herbs, monosodium glutamate, and other ingredients that are unwanted when cooking from scratch with fresh ingredients. Only pure bread crumbs—those without flavorings—are suitable.

Dried bread can be easily pulverized in a food processor or blender or with a hand grater. Use dense (not airy) Italian or other white so-called peasant bread containing no sugar, herbs, or flavorings. If using a food processor or blender, break up the dried bread into small pieces before grinding. After pulverizing into crumbs, pass the crumbs through a sieve to separate the large from the fine. Discard the coarse pieces and store the fine crumbs in a closed glass jar or container in the pantry. Bread absorbs moisture, so it is important to keep crumbs in a dry place—not in the refrigerator.

Most recipes direct you to toast the crumbs lightly before using to prevent them from absorbing oil too easily. The easiest way to do this is in a heavy skillet over medium heat. Stir the crumbs occasionally with a wooden spoon in order to toast them lightly and evenly, and watch them carefully, as they burn easily.

CHEESES, IN ITALIAN, **FORMAGGI.** Cheeses are important elements of the vegetarian table, both for eating and for cooking. They can be served before the meal as *antipasti*, but they are more typically brought out after the meal, with or without fresh fruit. Fresh cheeses served at these junctures are customarily drizzled with flavorful extra-virgin olive oil and sprinkled with freshly ground black pepper.

*Fontina*, a Piedmontese cheese with a history of five hundred years behind it, is made with great skill and care. A semi-soft, nutty, somewhat sweet cheese made from cow's milk, *fontina* is used extensively in the northern Italian kitchen. It is a good melting cheese, and consequently ideal as a topping for baked dishes.

*Gorgonzola* is characterized by the blue-green veins that run through it and by its pungent, barnyard aroma. A young *gorgonzola*, such as a *dolcelatte*, is relatively mild, creamy, and sweet. As it ages, it becomes *piccante*, spicy, and quite strong. Aged *gorgonzola* can be added to a green salad dressed with olive oil and wine vinegar. Mild *gorgonzola* makes an exceptional sauce for pasta and potato *gnocchi* when it is combined with butter, cream, and *parmigiano*. Like other perishable fresh cheeses, *gorgonzola* should be eaten within a day or two of purchase.

*Groviera*, Italian for *gruyère*, the French cheese, is used in northern Italian cooking, often in conjuction with other cheeses. It is especially useful combined with milder cheeses to create a complex flavor.

*Mozzarella* is a fresh, soft cheese that should be eaten on the same day it is made, still warm from the cheesemaker's kettle and dripping wet. Sadly, most Americans haven't had the opportunity to taste this remarkable culinary delight, which is not to be compared in any way with the industrially made mozzarella sold in supermarkets. True mozzarella is made from the milk of the water buffalo, but is seldom exported to this country because it sours rapidly. Cow's milk mozzarella is called *fior di latte,* or "flower of milk." Many Italian specialty shops in this country make cow's milk mozzarella daily. (Ignore the salt-free variety; this is an American phenomenon and is virtually tasteless.) According to mozzarella makers, to be true mozzarella the cheese must be eaten on the day it is made. After that, it is considered *scamorza,* a firmer cheese with more merit as a cooking cheese than an eating cheese.

*Parmigiano-reggiano* has many pretenders, but there is no substitute for the authentic handmade cheese from the region of Emilia-Romagna. A cow's milk cheese made with great skill and seven hundred years of know-how, *parmigiano* is aged for eighteen months to four years. The longer it ages, the more the flavor of the cheese intensifies. *Parmigiano* is always thought of as a grating cheese in America, but the Italians serve it as a table cheese, usually at the end of the meal with pears, grapes, or other fresh fruit. Young *parmigiano* is considered the best table cheese, while a *parmigiano* of three years is meant for grating and sprinkling on soups; on pastas, primarily those with butter-based sauces; and on *risotti.* *Parmigiano* of four years is used in stuffed-pasta fillings, stuffings for vegetables, and the like.

You will know the authentic cheese by the markings on its rind. Many specialty shops precut it and wrap it in plastic, but this method of storing cheeses prevents it from breathing properly. Search out a reputable cheese monger who will cut off a chunk for you from a huge wheel when you are ready to buy. Always ask for a taste. If the cheese is dry and crumbly, and whitish instead of golden, tender, and fragant, it has not been stored properly and has lost its unique properties. The best *parmigiano-reggiano* is strong in flavor, but it is a complex, mellow flavor. It is firm, but when cut, it flakes. Never, ever use imitation *parmigiano* sold in bottles and cans.

When cooking with *parmigiano,* it is important to remember that the less heat to which it is exposed, the better. Heat damages the cheese's unique flavor. This is especially true of the more aged *formaggi.* If the cheese becomes stringy when heated, it is too young for cooking. When adding it to soups, risotti, or pastas, sprinkle it on at the last minute. With some exceptions, *parmigiano* was traditionally used in butter-based dishes, and not in those containing olive oil. But today, with the increased use of olive oil, this is no longer a steadfast rule.

After going through the trouble to obtain authentic *parmigiano* and storing it properly (see page 17) be sure you insure its genuine flavor at the table by grating it only when you need it. Pregrating cheeses causes them to lose a great deal of their character. The best method for grating *parmigiano* is on the next-to-smallest holes on a regular box grater, or with a mini hand-cranked rotary grater. Grinding *parmigiano* in a food processor can be practical when the cheese is destined for use in fillings, but the results are too grainy for use in cream sauces or for topping pasta or *risotto.* The rinds that remain should never be thrown away. Store them in foil or waxed paper in the cheese drawer of a refrigerator and add them to *minestrone* or other soups for flavor. After being softened by the heat and moisture of the soup, they are delicious for nibbling on.

*Pecorino,* sheep's milk cheese, is the primary cheese in southern Italian cooking. This is saltier, sharper, and less rounded than *parmigiano-reggiano,* and should not be substituted for it. What is exported to America are the harder varieties from Lazio (of which Rome is the capital city) and Sardinia, and an excellent semisoft sheep cheese from Umbria and Tuscany, called *caciotta* in this country. *Pecorino romano* is probably the best sheep's milk cheese exported here, although *caciotta di Siena* can often be found in well-stocked cheese markets. *Fior di Sardegna*, a semisoft Sardinian sheep cheese useful in southern Italian cooking, is exported in small quantities. Young, mild *pecorino* has many uses in vegetarian cooking, particularly in certain baked dishes where a melting cheese is necessary but where mozzarella would be too bland. Numerous recipes here call for a semisoft *pecorino* such as Tuscan *caciotta* and *fior di Sardegna*. Do not attempt to substitute aged *pecorino* for its young relatives in recipes that call for the latter; it is too sharp for these purposes. Although not as refined as *parmigiano-reggiano*, young, mild *pecorino* also makes a good table cheese.

STORING CHEESES. Cheeses are living, and so they perish quickly. They are best eaten as soon as possible after purchase. If they have been stored in the refrigerator, they should be left for an hour at room temperature before serving for the best flavor. But do not allow them to remain at room temperature for more than several hours, or they will become oily. Set out only as much as will be eaten. Fresh cheeses such as mozzarella should be eaten as soon after they are made as possible because they quickly sour. Under refrigeration their delicate flavor is lost and their creamy texture altered, so it is best to purchase them on the same day they are to be eaten. *Parmigiano-reggiano* and *pecorino* age and their flavor intensifies even as they are stored in the refrigerator. Nonetheless, they should be used soon after purchase, and not kept in the refrigerator indefinitely.

To keep cheeses, wrap them in slightly dampened paper and then in a damp cloth towel or cheesecloth, or in waxed paper, and store in the refrigerator. Be sure there are no openings or tears in the paper. This method will keep hard cheeses such as *parmigiano* fresh and moist. While most shops use plastic wrap for storing cheeses because it is convenient, this is a mistake. Plastic does not allow cheese to breathe.

All fresh cheeses, including mozzarella and *gorgonzola*, lose flavor and some of their lovely creamy texture under refrigeration. If they must be kept past the day of purchase, wrap them in foil and store in a cool place. Mozzarella, if it is to be used as a cooking cheese rather than an eating cheese, can be frozen for several months.

MUSHROOMS, IN ITALIAN, FUNGHI. Cultivated mushrooms are not interchangeable with either fresh or dried wild mushrooms. Of all the wild mushrooms, *porcini*, *Boletus edulis* in Latin and known as *cèpes* in France, are the most prized in Italian cooking. They are immensely flavorful with a rich, bosky aroma that is positively intoxicating. The mushrooms grow under broad-leafed trees such as chestnut, oak, poplar, and hazelnut, and sometimes reach enormous size. (These wild *porcini* grow so large in Italy that they are eaten as a main course, sautéed in olive oil with garlic and fresh parsley, each cap the size of a steak, or as *cappelle di porcini al forno*, roasted whole in the oven.) The fabled *porcini* are only occasionally seen in specialty markets.

Other mushroom varieties that are gathered in the wild and found in season in specialty markets—particularly in the Pacific Northwest where the climate is conducive to mushrooms—include the *chanterelle* (golden, white, and black varieties), which has a delicate, apricoty flavor; black trumpet; wood ear (also cloud ear or tree ear); hen-of-the-woods (or *maitake*), which must be young, or it is too woody to eat; cauliflower mushroom; lobster mushroom; horn of plenty (also known as *trompette de la mort*, "trumpet of death"); chicken mushroom; *morel*, which is reminiscent of green pepper and caraway; and the glorious Japanese *matsutake* (or pine mushroom), which grows as large as a *porcino* and can be treated as a

cutlet such as in the recipe for *cotolette di funghi* on page 118. Some varieties of wild mushrooms are now cultivated. While they cannot be compared in flavor or aroma with those that are foraged, and their textures are generally softer and moister once cooked, they are lower in price and certainly worthy of culinary consideration. Mushrooms in this category include *shiitakes*, which have a firm, meatlike texture; golden oaks, a variety of *chanterelle* that is larger than its wild relative and also blander; oyster mushrooms (also called white trumpets), sometimes referred to as "veal mushrooms" by purveyors because of their tender texture, mild flavor, and versatility in cooking; forest corals (also called *Pom Pom Blanc*); enokitakes (or simply *enokis*); *honshimeji; cremini* (also known as Roman mushrooms, *prataioli*, or field mushrooms); and *portobellos*, which are full-grown *cremini*. While most of these mushroom varieties, cultivated and wild, are not found in Italy, they can used with great success in Italian recipes.

In buying mushrooms, avoid those that are bruised or have become damp or discolored from improper storage. To store, place them in a slightly dampened paper bag or damp (not wet) cloth towel in the refrigerator. Or keep them in a basket made of natural material, covered with a damp cloth towel. Never wrap in plastic; without air, moisture becomes trapped, making the mushrooms slimy.

To clean fresh mushrooms, brush them with a soft brush to remove dirt or sand. Washing them alters their texture, so they should not be immersed in water. If they are excessively gritty, the caps can be passed quickly under a jet of cold water. Do not, however, wet the gills, or undersides. Cut off tough or woody stems or stem tips. Do not peel mushrooms.

Dried *porcini* mushrooms, in Italian, *funghi porcini secchi*. Dried *funghi porcini* are the most practical alternative for the hard-to-find fresh *porcini*. Drying concentrates their extraordinary flavor. Using a small amount in sauces adds enormous flavor. Dried *porcini* can be added to fresh wild or cultivated mushrooms to boost the flavor of a sauce. Buy only the fleshy, predominantly light-colored part of the mushroom, not the small, dark, gnarled pieces, which are not as good. To rehydrate, soak the dried *porcini* in hot or boiling water for at least 20 minutes. Use only as much water as is necessary to cover them completely—about four times the volume of the dried mushrooms. Drain the mushrooms, then strain the soaking liquid through cheesecloth, a paper towel, or a fine sieve. This startlingly tasty liquor is usually added to the dish along with the mushrooms. If not, it can be stored in the refrigerator for several days, or frozen, and used to flavor other dishes in which mushroom flavor would be welcome.

Dried *chanterelles* and *morels* are often found next to dried *porcini* in food specialty shops. While they are cheaper, their flavor cannot compare to that of dried *porcini*.

OLIVE OIL, IN ITALIAN, **OLIO DI OLIVA**. Extra-virgin olive oil is indispensable in Italian cooking. Just a few years ago, only industrial quality, chemically treated, bland olive oils were available here, which made reproducing many authentic Italian dishes impossible. But now, extra-virgin olive oil is stocked even in supermarkets.

The terms *extra-virgin* and *cold pressed* refer to the oil released from the first pressing of young olives that have just started to turn green. (If the olives are too mature, their acidity level is too high.) This oil is aromatic, richly flavored from the fruity essence of the olive, and a warm, glowing green, green-gold, or deep gold.

Only perfect, unbruised olives that have never fallen to the ground are used in making this oil. In the best traditional method of making oil, these olives are stone-ground and the oil extracted without the use of chemicals. As with other quality Italian products, the process is labor-intensive and largely done by hand. Consequently, high-grade extra-virgin olive oil is both rare and expensive: Its average cost is double or even triple that of industrially produced, chemically treated oils also labeled "extra-virgin." Producers of high-grade extra-virgin olive oil claim that only 20 percent of oils so-labeled are, in fact, the genuine article.

The paste that remains after the first pressing of the olives must be treated chemically in order to distill it; the process results in a blander, cheaper grade of olive oil. Despite its chemical additives, it is often labeled "pure olive oil." Producers mix some extra-virgin oil with it to add flavor and aroma, but its use is limited to that of all-purpose cooking oil.

Extra-virgin olive oil, on the other hand, is used as a condiment as well as a cooking oil. The best way to experience its full, clear taste is to use it cold. For example, in Sardinia it is sprinkled on the famous *carta di musica* (also called *fogli di musica*, or *pane carasau*), crisp, unleavened, paper-thin flatbread, and throughout Italy on fresh bread or toasted bread. It is drizzled over soups at the table for added flavor. One of the best olive oils I ever tasted was in Umbria, poured over a soup of puréed fava beans. That unforgettable oil turned a simple bowl of soup into an exquisite dish. A stream of extra-virgin oil is typically the sole flavoring applied to warm or cold beans, particularly in Tuscan cooking, and it anoints cooked vegetables, raw vegetables, and salads alike. It is used as liberally in Italian cooking as Americans have traditionally used butter.

Not all extra-virgin olive oils are equal, however. While the most well-known olive oil–producing regions are Apulia, Tuscany, and Liguria, olive oil is made in nearly all of Italy with the exception of the most northern areas of the country. The flavors of these many oils reflect the climate and soil of their regions, the stage at which the olives were harvested, and the variety of olives from which they were derived. Tuscan oils are considered peppery, while the oils of Liguria have a reputation for being sweet. Oils from the south are often more pungent and darker; those from the northern regions are more delicate. The stronger flavor and heavier feel of southern oils reflect the lower rainfall of those regions, and thus the lower water content in the olives. But these generalities don't always apply. Suffice it to say that the oils of each region and even each estate are unique. Even color is not in any way a barometer of flavor.

The different flavors of various extra-virgin olive oils make them suitable for different types of dishes. For example, "sweet" oils are ideally used for making mayonnaise, for salads, and for foods with subtle flavors. Stronger-flavored oils are more appropriate for use in garlicky tomato sauces, for *bruschetta* (garlic toast), and for many robust southern Italian dishes. Oils that fall in between these two categories are compatible with raw, boiled, and steamed vegetables, and for sprinkling on vegetable soups.

Oil marked "estate bottled" indicates an artisan-produced oil made from olives of a single estate rather than from fruits purchased from numerous outside producers and blended. These oils are more costly than others, but are bound to be better. The true test is in the tasting. The taste of good extra-virgin olive oil is reminiscent, perhaps more than anything else, of artichokes. Other adjectives used to describe its flavors and aromas include grassy, vegetal, and almondy. The best way to select olive oil is to try different producers and decide for yourself which oil you like. Compare the more costly ones with the cheaper ones, remembering that a bottle of oil will go a long way in compar-

ison to an equally costly bottle of wine, which would be consumed in one meal.

I like the fruitiness and aroma of unfiltered first-pressed oil for use as a condiment. One must take care with unfiltered oils, however. Their higher fruit content causes them to turn rancid more quickly than filtered oil. They should be used frequently, not stored away like precious wine. Most extra-virgin olive oils are filtered both to protect them from spoiling and to expel impurities.

Although heating extra-virgin olive oil causes it to lose some of its unique characteristics, it is incomparable in cooking because of the flavor it imparts to food. Only extra-virgin olive oil should be used in dressings; no others will do. I have indicated throughout this book where it is essential to use extra-virgin olive oil. In other recipes, it should be used if it is affordable; otherwise substitute virgin olive oil, which is obtained by blending extra-virgin olive oil and so-called pure olive oil. For frying, use pure olive oil unless vegetable oil is suggested as an alternative.

Olive oil is at its best when it is very young. As it ages it turns rancid. This is particularly true of extra-virgin olive oil because of its greater fruit content. Light and heat will cause it to deteriorate quickly. Sometimes olive oil sits on the shelf in the market far too long and spoils before it is ever sold. To prevent this, look for the vintage date on the bottle before buying extra-virgin olive oil and buy in small quantities from a store where merchandise moves quickly (keep in mind that the new vintage arrives every winter, usually around January). Manufacturers of high-grade extra-virgin olive oil try to protect the life of their oils by bottling them in dark green glass vessels. The dark glass prevents oxidation by filtering out light. But the best way to insure that oil remains fresh is to use it frequently.

To store olive oil, cap it and store it in a cool, dark place. It should not be refrigerated nor stored near a direct source of heat. Nor should you ever top oil with fresh oil from a new bottle. The life of olive oil is generally one year. If it is well conserved, it can last up to three years, although during that time it will become more intensely flavored.

### KNOWING HOW TO PURCHASE FRESH VEGETABLES

One way to insure the vegetables you buy have flavor is to buy them when they are in season. Everyone knows that tomatoes grown in hothouses, no matter how good they look, simply do not have the taste and aroma of tomatoes that grow and ripen under the sun. This applies to all vegetables.

As much as possible, purchase vegetables straight from the farm. Locally grown fruits and vegetables will have traveled far fewer miles to reach you, which means it is less likely they have been exposed to the chemicals some agricultural operations use to extend the shelf life of produce that travels great distances. In addition, locally produced vegetables probably go through fewer hands before you see them, and have consequently been mishandled far less. They may also cost less.

In general, when choosing vegetables, be sure they are not bruised, discolored, spotty, wilted, or wrinkled. Truly fresh vegetables are moist and crisp, not dried out and limp. Leafy vegetables should show not even a hint of yellowed leaves. Once you purchase them, use them. The longer vegetables are stored, the more flavor and nutritive value they lose.

Virtually all vegetables suffer diminished flavor and texture when they are overly mature. In large artichokes, for example, the hairy choke is too developed, and the heart is tough and lacking taste; when the leaves are open like a dying rose rather than sleek and tight against one another, the thistle is past its prime. Carrots that are grown too large are woody at their core, as well as lacking in sweetness. Zucchini and many other squashes are virtually useless when allowed to grow too large: The skin toughens and turns bitter, the seeds enlarge so much that they have to be removed, and the flesh of the squash loses its sweetness and crispness. The ideal size for zucchini and yellow summer squashes is six to eight ounces. One of the simplest and most delicious ways to eat zucchini is to procure them when they are no larger than this, boil them whole in salted water until they are tender, and eat them anointed simply with good extra-virgin olive oil and a squeeze of fresh lemon juice.

On the other hand, vegetables need to grow large enough to develop fully their inherent flavor. Undergrown vegetables are as useless as overgrown ones. In the 1980s, when baby vegetables were the rage, they were often picked when so immature they were too bitter to eat. During that era I left many an adorable baby vegetable on my plate in fashionable restaurants because they were virtually inedible.

*Finocchio*, or fresh fennel, is still relatively uncommon, although it is not difficult to find in the early autumn when it is in season. The secret to selecting the sweetest fennel is to know the gender of the bulb. Somewhat flat bulbs are males and are not as sweet as the females, which are rounder.

When choosing tomatoes, always remember that various types of tomatoes are grown for different purposes. Plum tomatoes have few seeds, are fleshy and compact, and contain less water than other varieties. These characteristics make them ideal for sauces. Large American beefsteak tomatoes, while tasty when allowed to grow and ripen in their natural season, have a higher water content and are not as suitable for sauces. When other tomato varieties disappoint, cherry tomatoes, which are often quite sweet, can be used in recipes calling for fresh tomatoes, although peeling and seeding takes considerable time and patience. Tomatoes should be stored at room temperature. Refrigerating them alters their flavor. Once peeled and seeded for use in a sauce, they can be frozen for up to three months. To accelerate ripening, wrap tomatoes in newspaper and store them in a warm spot (about 70 degrees F). To hold tomatoes, store them in a dark, humid (but not damp), cool place (55 to 60 degrees F). Place them so that they do not touch one another, such as on a rack or shelving that allows circulation.

When good fresh tomatoes are not available, using good canned tomatoes is critical for successful results. The best canned tomatoes are the imported Italian San Marzano variety that are packed whole, in their own juices. In recent years, however, I have come across several domestic brands of canned plum tomatoes that are excellent.

Individual recipes in all the chapters give further guidance on selecting as well as preparing vegetables.

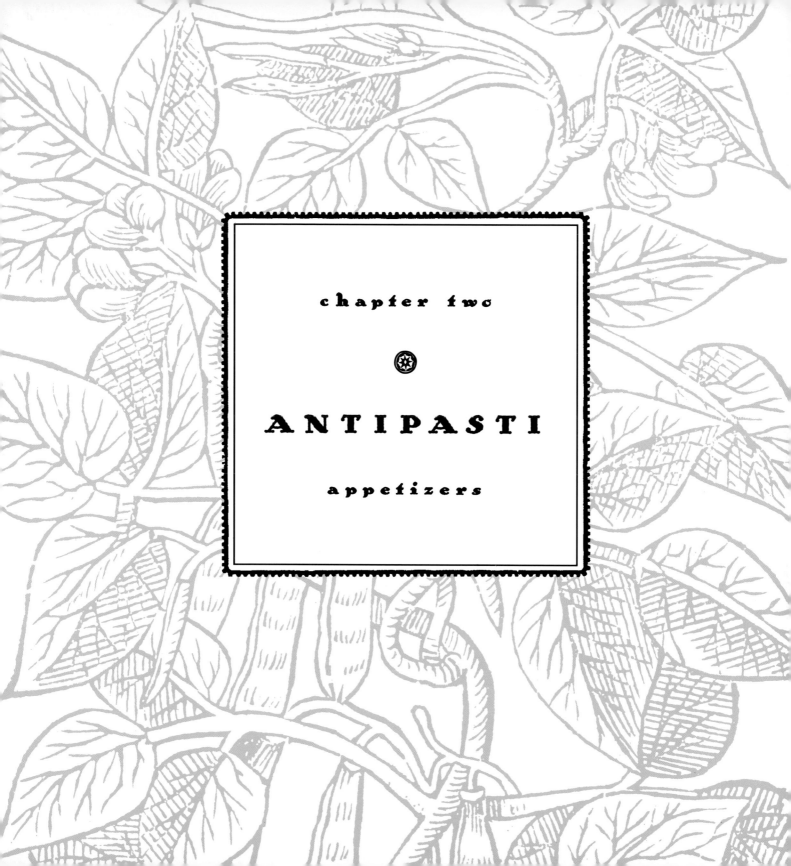

chapter two

ANTIPASTI

appetizers

**W**HEN I WROTE **ANTIPASTI: THE LITTLE DISHES OF ITALY,** I HAD MANY MORE RECIPES THAN COULD BE CONTAINED IN THE VOLUME. HAPPILY, I NOW HAVE ANOTHER OPPORTUNITY TO ADD A FEW MORE TO MY READERS' REPERTOIRES.

These little dishes are perhaps the most lighthearted of all Italian recipes. They are like the kisses that are the prelude to a great love affair: beguiling, enticing, promising. They are the flavors, aromas, and colors of the Italian table in miniature.

This course before the main meal has typically been a part of restaurant dining, or reserved for holidays and other celebrations. In past times, it played a role in the daily eating habits of wealthier households rather than that of peasant abodes. But these small dishes have become more popular in the last fifty years with the expansion of the middle class and the transition for many from country to city lifestyles.

*Antipasto*, literally "before the meal," once meant just that. But in today's *cucina*, *antipasti* play many roles. What is sometimes a *contorno*, a side dish of vegetables served with or after the main course, might appear on the *antipasto* table as well. Or an *antipasto* might comprise, either alone or in combination with other starters, a whole meal. Vegetable appetizers in particular, because of their lightness, compatibility with many meat and nonmeat courses, and ease of preparation, easily fit into appetizer, first-course, or side-dish categories.

Where once the word *antipasti* was synonymous in American-Italian restaurants with an inauthentic assortment of *salame*, pickled vegetables, nondescript olives, and maybe a cheese or two served on a platter, restaurant goers can now expect to be served such *antipasti* as little *focacce* (savory flatbreads), delectable roasted vegetables, and marinated *bocconcini* (fresh mozzarella dressed with extra-virgin olive oil and fresh basil) in restaurants that are commited to offering authentic Italian food. Many of these dishes are simple to prepare and hardly require a recipe. But what makes them so delicious, and often so elusive outside of Italy, is the quality and freshness of ingredients—the use of *parmigiano-reggiano*, of imported extra-virgin olive oil and olives, and so on. These factors should not be barriers to reproducing excellent Italian dishes at home in America, however. One has only to commit oneself to buying fresh vegetables and high-quality imported and domestic products whenever possible.

What I offer here is just a sampling of *antipasti* possibilities. While *pizzette, focaccia,* and other savory breads and pies could fall into the *antipasto* category, I have chosen to focus on the treatment of vegetables starters. Thus there are recipes for stuffed vegetables of many varieties; cooked vegetable salads and a delightful rice and asparagus salad from the Piedmont; *crostini*—toasted bread or *polenta*—with various vegetable toppings; three classic methods for deep-frying vegetables (something the Italians do so very well); and pickled vegetables.

# UOVA RIPIENE AL LIMONE

### LEMON-FLAVORED STUFFED EGGS

#### FOR 8 PEOPLE

WHAT MAKES THESE EGGS SO GOOD IS THE HOMEMADE MAYONNAISE THAT BINDS THE STUFFING. IT IS EASY TO MAKE IN A BLENDER, AS LONG AS ONE REMEMBERS TO BRING ALL THE INGREDIENTS AND THE TOOLS TO ROOM TEMPERATURE BEFORE PROCEEDING, AND TO ADD THE OIL LITTLE BY LITTLE. A FOOD PROCESSOR CAN BE USED SUCCESSFULLY IF MAKING LARGER AMOUNTS.

Place the eggs in a saucepan, cover with cold water, and bring to a boil. Reduce the heat to medium-low to prevent the eggs from knocking against each other as they cook. Cook for 7 minutes.

Meanwhile, in a blender, make the mayonnaise. Place the oil in a small pitcher. Crack the egg into the jar of the blender and blend briefly to beat lightly. Add 2 tablespoons of the oil. Blend on high speed for 10 seconds. With the machine on the same setting, add the oil drop by drop, then when the mixture becomes creamy, continue adding the oil in a very thin, slow, steady stream. It is crucial not to add too much oil at once or the mayonnaise will not emulsify. Turn off the blender motor. Use a rubber spatula to scrape the inside of the blender jar so that all the ingredients are thoroughly combined. Stir the salt into the lemon juice and add it with the mustard and pepper. Engage the blender again to combine thoroughly, about 30 seconds. You will have about 1 cup mayonnaise. Remove 5 tablespoons to use for adding to the stuffing. Cover and refrigerate the remaining mayonnaise; it will keep for a week.

When the eggs are ready, rinse them under cold water to cool them, then remove their shells. Cut each egg in half lengthwise. Carefully remove the hard-cooked yolks and place them in a blender or food processor. Set the egg whites aside. To the yolks, add the 5 tablespoons mayonnaise, the lemon zest, and salt to taste, and whip until smooth, only several seconds.

Using a teaspoon, place a mound of the mixture into the well of each egg white. Scatter some capers on the top of each and sprinkle with the pepper. Serve at room temperature.

*8 eggs*

*For the mayonnaise:*
*¾ cup olive oil*
*1 egg, at room temperature*
*½ teaspoon salt, or to taste*
*2 tablespoons freshly squeezed lemon juice, or to taste*
*½ teaspoon Dijon-style mustard*
*dash of freshly milled white pepper*

*5 tablespoons mayonnaise*
*zest of 1 large lemon*
*salt*
*1 tablespoon drained small capers*
*cayenne pepper or freshly milled white pepper*

# CARCIOFI ALL'ISOLA

✺

FRIED BABY ARTICHOKES

FOR 3 PEOPLE

THIS IS ONE OF THE MOST COMMON WAYS TO COOK ARTICHOKES, BUT IT IS NOT WORTH DOING UNLESS THE ARTICHOKES ARE SMALL, TENDER, AND FRESH. TRULY FRESH ARTICHOKES ARE RARE IN AMERICAN MARKETS, BUT I INCLUDE THIS RECIPE FOR THOSE WHO CHANCE UPON THEM, BECAUSE IT IS ONE OF THE SIMPLEST AND MOST DELICIOUS WAYS OF COOKING THEM. ONE OF MY FAVORITE NEIGHBORHOOD RESTAURANTS, ISOLA, ON MANHATTAN'S UPPER WEST SIDE, DOES A MARVELOUS JOB WITH THEM, AND KEEPS THEM ON THE MENU EVEN THOUGH THERE IS NOT MUCH PROFIT BY THE TIME THEY'VE BOUGHT THE ARTICHOKES AND FRIED THEM IN EXTRA-VIRGIN OLIVE OIL.

*juice of 1 lemon*
*6 baby artichokes*
*extra-virgin olive oil or olive oil for*
*    frying*
*3 cloves garlic, unpeeled, bruised*
*sea salt*

Have ready a large glass or ceramic bowl (do not use metal) filled with cold water to which you have added the lemon juice. Clean the artichokes according to the directions on page 119, but remember that because baby artichokes are more tender, there will be fewer tough outer leaves to remove. Then cut each of the artichokes lengthwise into quarters or into slices ¼ inch thick. Immediately put the cleaned artichokes into the waiting acidulated water to prevent them from turning brown. Leave them in the water until you are ready to fry them. (Once cleaned, the artichoke hearts can remain in the water-and-lemon bath in the refrigerator for up to 24 hours.)

In a large skillet, pour in oil to a depth of about ¼ inch. Place the garlic in the oil and warm it over medium heat. Meanwhile, drain the artichokes and, using a clean kitchen towel or paper towels, dry them thoroughly. Add the artichokes to the oil, taking care not to crowd the pan and thus bring down the temperature of the oil. The garlic cloves should remain until they have browned, then remove and discard them. Fry the artichoke slices over medium heat on both sides, turning once, until they are golden, 10 to 15 minutes. Now dip your hand in cold water and, keeping a safe distance from the pan, splatter cold water over the artichokes. Do this twice, the second time right after the first. Cook until the artichokes are golden brown and crisp, about 5 minutes longer.

Using a slotted spoon, remove to paper towels to drain briefly. Sprinkle with salt to taste, and serve piping hot.

# FUNGHI RIPIENI

❀

STUFFED MUSHROOMS

FOR 3 PEOPLE

**M**USHROOMS ARE OFTEN STUFFED WITH SAUSAGE, **PROSCIUTTO**, OR GROUND MEAT IN THE ITALIAN KITCHEN, BUT THIS CLASSIC VEGETARIAN STUFFING IS VERY FLAVORFUL. IN ITALY, **PORCINI** ARE USED, BUT THIS DISH CAN BE MADE WITH CULTIVATED MUSHROOMS, INCLUDING **CREMINI** OR **PORTOBELLOS**.

*12 fresh cultivated mushrooms at least 2 inches in diameter (about ¾ pound total weight)*

*2 tablespoons extra-virgin olive oil, plus additional olive oil for drizzling*

*2 green onions, including 1 inch of green tops, chopped*

*2 large cloves garlic, finely chopped or passed through a garlic press*

*2–½ tablespoons chopped fresh Italian parsley*

*¼ cup fine dried bread crumbs*

*3 tablespoons freshly grated parmigiano*

*½ teaspoon minced fresh oregano, or ¼ teaspoon dried oregano*

*¼ teaspoon salt*

*freshly milled black pepper*

*1 tablespoon dry white wine*

Preheat an oven to 375 degrees F. Using a soft brush or clean kitchen towel, remove any dirt from the mushrooms. Do not wash them because water alters their texture. Trim off the tough bottom from each stem and discard; only the rest of the stem will be used. Separate the stems at the base of the caps of 9 of the mushrooms. Chop all of the stems along with the 3 remaining whole mushrooms.

In a skillet over medium heat, warm the 2 tablespoons olive oil. Add the onions, garlic, and parsley and sauté gently until wilted, about 4 minutes. Add the chopped mushrooms and sauté gently until softened, about 5 more minutes. Remove the mixture to a small bowl. Add the bread crumbs, *parmigiano*, oregano, salt, and pepper to taste to the mushroom mixture and mix well.

Fill each mushroom cap with an equal amount of the stuffing, using your hands to form the stuffing into a nice even mound and to push it down to fill the underside of the caps. Place the filled mushrooms on a baking sheet. Sprinkle the wine evenly over the mushrooms, and then drizzle each mushroom very lightly with olive oil.

Cover loosely with aluminum foil and bake for 20 minutes. Remove the foil and bake until the mushrooms are bubbling and golden, an additional 10 to 15 minutes. Serve hot or warm.

AHEAD-OF-TIME NOTE: The mushrooms can be stuffed up to a day in advance of serving, covered, and refrigerated until ready to bake. Sprinkle with the wine and olive oil just before baking.

# INSALATA DI PEPERONI ARROSTITI ALLA PIEMONTESE

❀

SALAD OF ROASTED PEPPERS, OLIVES, AND FONTINA, PIEDMONT STYLE

FOR 4 PEOPLE

THE CUISINE OF PIEDMONT INCLUDES NUMEROUS INTERESTING COOKED VEGETABLE SALADS THAT ARE SERVED AS STARTERS, AND THIS IS ONE OF THEM. RED BELL PEPPERS CAN ALSO BE USED, BUT I LOVE THE AESTHETICS OF THE YELLOW PEPPERS WITH THE DEEP GREEN OF THE OLIVES.

Arrange the peppers on a grill rack above a charcoal fire, on wire racks positioned over the burners of a gas or electric stove, 2 to 3 inches under a preheated broiler, or in an oven preheated to 400 degrees F. Roast them until they are charred all over and tender inside, turning them frequently to insure they blacken evenly, about 30 minutes in the oven, but less time by the other methods. Set aside to cool.

When the peppers are cool enough to handle, using your fingertips, peel off the skins. Cut the peppers in half and remove and discard the stems, ribs, and seeds. (Do not do this under running water; it will wash away some of the delicious smoky flavor.) Cut the peppers lengthwise into ½-inch-wide strips and place in a bowl. Add the oil, mustard, vinegar, salt and pepper to taste, olives, and cheese and toss gently to mix well. Serve at room temperature.

AHEAD-OF-TIME NOTE: This *antipasto* can be prepared several hours in advance of serving and kept at room temperature. It can also be made up to 3 days in advance, omitting the cheese, and refrigerated until the day of serving. Bring it to room temperature before serving and add the cheese up to several hours before serving.

*3 large yellow bell peppers*

*2 tablespoons extra-virgin olive oil*

*1 teaspoon Dijon-style mustard*

*1 teaspoon red wine vinegar*

*salt*

*freshly milled white pepper*

*2 tablespoons sliced, pitted imported green olives*

*¼ pound fontina, cut into long, thin strips*

# INSALATA DI RISO ALLA PIEMONTESE

❋

RICE SALAD, PIEDMONT STYLE

FOR 4 OR 5 PEOPLE

**R**ICE SALADS ARE FOUND IN MANY PARTS OF ITALY, AND THERE ARE MANY WAYS OF MAKING THEM. WHEREAS THEY OFTEN INCLUDE SHELLFISH, MOST COMMONLY SHRIMP, OR FLAKED CANNED TUNA, STRICTLY VEGETARIAN VERSIONS ARE RARE. THERE IS A GREATER PROPORTION OF OTHER INGREDIENTS TO RICE IN THESE SALADS, AND THERE SHOULD BE A MARKED CONTRAST BETWEEN THE TEXTURE OF THE RICE, WHICH ALTHOUGH IT MUST BE COOKED **AL DENTE**, IS STILL SOFT, AND THE OTHER INGREDIENTS, SOME OF WHICH SHOULD BE CRISP. RICE SALADS ARE GREAT BUFFET AND PLAN-AHEAD DISHES, AS THEY CAN BE PREPARED A FEW HOURS IN ADVANCE AND LEFT AT ROOM TEMPERATURE. ❋ HERE IS AN ADAPTATION OF A PIEDMONTESE RICE SALAD. IN THE ORIGINAL VERSION, THE RICE IS COOKED IN BROTH, NOT WATER, AND WHITE TRUFFLES ARE INCLUDED. I ADD **PINOLI** (PINE NUTS), A ROASTED RED PEPPER, AND FINELY SLICED GREEN ONION. CHEWY WILD MUSHROOMS, FIRST STEAMED BRIEFLY, THEN SEARED IN A SKILLET, PROVIDE A NICE TEXTURAL COUNTERPOINT TO BOTH THE TENDER RICE AND THE CRUNCHY VEGETABLES. I PREFER NOT TO MUDDLE FLAVORS BY COMBINING TOO MANY INGREDIENTS, BUT CERTAINLY PEAS COULD SUBSTITUTE FOR ASPARAGUS, SLICED ALMONDS FOR **PINOLI**, AND SLICED TOMATOES (SEEDS REMOVED) FOR ROASTED PEPPER. FLAVORFUL IMPORTED OLIVES CAN ALSO BE ADDED. MY FAVORITE COMBINATION, HOWEVER, IS THE ONE THAT FOLLOWS, A VERY PRETTY AND APPEALING DISH.

3 quarts water

¾ cup long-grain white rice

1 tablespoon salt

1 red bell pepper, or 1 bottled red sweet
    pepper

¾ pound fresh asparagus (9 to 12
    spears)

¼ pound fresh cap-and-stem variety
    wild mushrooms, such as porcini
    or shiitake

2 or 3 teaspoons olive oil

⅓ cup pinoli (pine nuts)

In a saucepan, bring the water to a boil and stir in the rice and salt. Cook until the rice is tender but firm, 12 to 15 minutes (cooking time could be much longer, depending upon the variety of rice). Drain the rice immediately into a strainer and then rinse it with cold running water. Drain it very well again.

Meanwhile, roast the bell pepper and peel, stem, seed, and derib, as directed on page 33. Cut into strips 2 inches long by ¼ inch wide. Alternatively, seed and derib the bottled pepper and cut into strips of the same dimensions. Set aside.

Trim the hard tips off the asparagus. Using a paring knife, peel the thicker skin at the base end of each asparagus stalk. (By paring away the thicker bottom skin, much of the stalk, which is tender under the tougher lower skin, is saved.) Arrange the asparagus on a steamer rack over a pan of boiling water. Cover and steam until the asparagus are just tender, 4 to 5 minutes; be careful not to damage the flowerlike buds at the top. Or in a skillet large enough to accommodate comfortably the length of the asparagus, bring enough salted water to cover the asparagus to a boil, add them to the water, and boil until tender but firm, 4 to 5 minutes. (Boiling them in salted water does not alter their bright green color as much as steaming does.) In either case, do not overcook them! Remove the asparagus from the steamer, or drain them immediately, and immerse in cold water to arrest cooking. Cut the asparagus crosswise on the diagonal into slices about ¾ inch long. Set aside.

To prepare the mushrooms, using a soft brush or clean kitchen towel, remove any dirt. Do not wash them because water alters their texture. Trim off the tough bottoms from the stems or remove the whole stems·if they are excessively woody. Place the cleaned whole mushrooms on a steamer rack over a pan of boiling water. Cover and steam until tender, about 4 minutes. Remove from the heat immediately and pat dry with a clean kitchen towel or paper towel. Cut them lengthwise into thin slices.

In a skillet, preferably nonstick, heat the 2 teaspoons of olive oil over high heat. If the skillet is not nonstick, use 3 teaspoons instead of 2 teaspoons oil. When the oil is extremely hot (hot enough to sear the mushrooms upon contact), add the sliced mushrooms and sear them on both sides, turning once; this will take 1 minute or less in total. Remove the mushrooms from the skillet immediately to prevent overcooking.

In a serving dish, combine the rice, pepper strips, asparagus, mushrooms, *pinoli*, celery or fennel and leaves or fronds, and onion. If these ingredients are still warm, all the better; the heat will bring out the flavor of the olive oil. In a small bowl, combine all the ingredients for the dressing and, using a fork or whisk, mix well. Pour the dressing over the salad ingredients and toss well. Taste and adjust the seasoning with salt, then serve at room temperature.

AHEAD-OF-TIME NOTE: This dish can be made up to 4 hours in advance of serving and kept at room temperature. It will become limp, however, if made too far in advance of serving.

1 small celery or fennel stalk, thinly
    sliced, including 1 tablespoon
    chopped young leaves or fronds
1 green onion, including 1 inch of the
    green tops, thinly sliced

*For the dressing:*
¼ cup extra-virgin olive oil
1 tablespoon white wine vinegar
¼ teaspoon Dijon-style mustard
½ yolk from 1 extra-large egg
¼ teaspoon salt, or to taste
freshly milled black or white pepper

# CAPONATA

❋

SWEET-AND-SOUR SICILIAN EGGPLANT COMPOTE

FOR 8 TO 10 PEOPLE

CAPONATA, SOMETIMES CALLED **CAPONATINA**, IS QUINTESSENTIALLY SICILIAN. THE ALLIANCE OF SWEET AND SOUR, NOT TYPICALLY FOUND IN ITALIAN COOKING EXCEPT IN VENETIAN CUISINE, HARKENS BACK TO THE SARACENS. THERE ARE NUMEROUS PROVINCIAL VARIATIONS OF **CAPONATA**. IN SOME VERSIONS, BITTER CHOCOLATE OR PINE NUTS ARE ADDED; IN STILL OTHERS BLACK RATHER THAN GREEN OLIVES ARE USED. THIS IS ONE OF THE MOST SIMPLE, AND MY FAVORITE VERSION. CELERY, SO OFTEN THE WALLFLOWER OF THE VEGETABLE GARDEN, IS TRIUMPHANT HERE. ITS LIGHTNESS, CRISP TEXTURE, AND LOVELY TRANSLUCENT GREEN COLOR ARE CRITICAL TO THIS COMPOTE OF RICH, CREAMY PURPLES. THE LARGE QUANTITY OF SAUTÉED ONION PROVIDES NECESSARY SWEETNESS, AN IMPORTANT BALANCE TO THE SOUR ELEMENTS IN THE COMPOTE. THE PUNCTUATIONS OF SALT, CAPERS, AND TART OLIVES GIVE THE DISH DELIGHTFUL ZEST. THE OLIVES SHOULD BE FLAVORFUL IMPORTED GREEN ONES, SUCH AS THOSE FROM SICILY. **PONENTINE** OLIVES OR GREEN GREEK OLIVES WILL ALSO DO. ❋ AN OLD ITALIAN VEGETABLE FARMER ONCE TOLD ME THAT MALE EGGPLANTS, WHICH CAN BE IDENTIFIED BY THEIR SMALLER NAVELS (AT THE BOTTOM OF THE EGGPLANT), CONTAIN FEWER BITTER SEEDS, AND I HAVE FOUND THIS TO BE TRUE. ALSO, ALWAYS SELECT EGGPLANTS THAT ARE FIRM, WITH NO BRUISES, SOFT SPOTS, OR WRINKLY SKIN.

*2 eggplants (about 1-½ pounds each)*

*salt for sprinkling on eggplants, plus 1 teaspoon salt*

*olive oil or vegetable oil for frying*

*2 large onions, cut into small dice*

*4 celery stalks, leaves removed, cut into small dice*

*½ cup pitted green olives, cut in half or quarters, depending upon olive size*

*¼ cup drained small capers*

*1 cup canned tomato sauce or strained tomato purée*

Leave the skins on the eggplants, but trim off and discard the stems and navels. Cut into 1-inch cubes. Place the eggplant cubes in a large colander and sprinkle with salt. Place the colander in the sink or over a dish and let stand so the bitter liquid drains out of the seeds, 30 to 40 minutes. Rinse under cold water and pat dry thoroughly with clean kitchen towels. Set aside.

In a large skillet over medium heat, pour in oil to a depth of 1 inch. When the oil is hot enough to make the eggplant sizzle (375 degrees F), fry the eggplant in batches, leaving enough space around the cubes to prevent overcrowding. Fry until golden on both sides, about 10 minutes. Using a slotted spoon, remove to paper towels to drain. Continue in this manner until all the eggplant cubes have been fried and drained. Transfer the fried eggplant to a large serving bowl. Filter the oil for reuse.

In a medium skillet over moderate heat, warm 2 tablespoons of the frying oil.

Add the onions and sauté until they are translucent but not colored, 3 to 4 minutes. Remove from the pan with a slotted spoon and add to the bowl with the eggplant.

Heat another 2 tablespoons of the reserved oil in the same skillet over medium heat. Add the celery and sauté until it sweats, 4 to 5 minutes. Do not overcook the celery; it should be cooked but still crisp. Remove from the pan with a slotted spoon and add to the bowl with the other vegetables. Add the olives and capers to the bowl, too.

Add the tomato sauce or purée to the same skillet and heat it just until it begins to simmer. Add the vinegar, sugar, the 1 teaspoon salt, and the pepper and heat until the mixture begins to simmer again. Remove from the heat and add to the vegetables in the bowl. Mix well. Taste and adjust the seasoning with salt.

Serve at room temperature.

AHEAD-OF-TIME NOTE: This dish can be prepared up to 5 days in advance and refrigerated. Bring it to room temperature before serving. The longer the vegetables marinate in the vinegary sauce, the sharper their flavor becomes.

½ cup red wine vinegar

1-½ tablespoons sugar

¼ teaspoon freshly milled black pepper, or to taste

# MELANZANE IN INSALATA ALLA CALABRESE

✽

EGGPLANT SALAD, CALABRIA STYLE

FOR 4 PEOPLE

THE USE OF MINT IN THIS RECIPE IS REMINISCENT OF THE WAY EGGPLANT IS TYPICALLY PREPARED IN THE LEVANT. INDEED, SUCH AN INFLUENCE IS NOT SURPRISING IN CALABRIA AND OTHER PARTS OF THE ITALIAN SOUTH, WHERE GREEKS AND SARACENS ESTABLISHED A LASTING GASTRONOMICAL FOUNDATION. ✽ IN THIS CALABRIAN RECIPE, THE SKIN IS LEFT ON THE EGGPLANT. THIS IS RATHER NICE BECAUSE IT HAS A PLEASANT TASTE, TEXTURE, AND COLOR AFTER COOKING. IN SOME VERSIONS, THE GARLIC IS NOT COOKED IN THE EGGPLANT; RATHER, IT IS CHOPPED RAW AND ADDED TO THE COOKED EGGPLANT WITH THE DRESSING. THIS IS VERY MUCH A MATTER OF PERSONAL PREFERENCE. I LIKE TO BAKE THE GARLIC INSIDE THE EGGPLANT BECAUSE COOKING SOFTENS AND SWEETENS IT.

*1 eggplant (about 1 pound)*

*salt for sprinkling on eggplant, plus ½ teaspoon salt*

*extra-virgin olive oil for oiling baking sheet, plus 2 teaspoons olive oil*

*2 large cloves garlic, sliced lengthwise into slivers*

*1-½ teaspoons red wine vinegar*

*2 teaspoons chopped fresh mint, 1 teaspoon crumbled dried mint, or 2 teaspoons chopped fresh Italian parsley*

*pinch of red pepper flakes, or to taste*

Leave the skin on the eggplant, but trim off and discard the stem and navel. Cut the eggplant in half lengthwise. Make slashes about ½ inch deep in their flesh on the cut sides and sprinkle with salt. Place the halves cut sides down in a colander. Place the colander in the sink or over a dish and let stand so the bitter liquid drains out of the seeds, about 40 minutes.

Meanwhile, preheat an oven to 400 degrees F. Cover a baking sheet with aluminum foil and oil it lightly.

Rinse the eggplant under cold water and pat thoroughly dry with clean kitchen towels. Slip the garlic slivers into the slashes in the eggplant. Place the eggplant halves cut sides down on the foil-lined sheet. Cover loosely with more foil and bake until completely tender when pierced with a knife, about 20 minutes.

Remove the eggplant from the oven and let cool somewhat until it can be handled, then cut into dice no larger than approximately 1 inch. (Do not remove the skin.) The garlic will have softened and sweetened during cooking; do not remove it. Place in a serving bowl. Add the 2 teaspoons olive oil, the vinegar, the ½ teaspoon salt, the mint, and the pepper flakes and toss well. Taste and adjust the seasoning.

Serve at room temperature.

# MELANZANE RIPIENE
# ALLA BASILICATA

❊

STUFFED EGGPLANT, BASILICATA STYLE

FOR 4 PEOPLE

HERE IS ONE OF THE MANY WAYS EGGPLANTS ARE STUFFED IN THE CAMPANIA AND BASILICATA REGIONS. THE METHOD IS PROBABLY ONE OF THE SIMPLEST FOR STUFFING VEGETABLES BECAUSE THE EGGPLANT PULP IS NOT REMOVED. INSTEAD, THE FLESH IS SCORED AND A SAVORY BREAD CRUMB MIXTURE IS WORKED INTO THE SLASHES; THE REMAINING CRUMB MIXTURE IS THEN SPREAD ON TOP BEFORE BAKING. THE EGGPLANTS SHOULD BE SMALL, TENDER ONES. EITHER SMALL GLOBULAR ITALIAN EGGPLANTS OR THE COMPARATIVELY SEEDLESS SLENDER JAPANESE EGGPLANTS CAN BE USED.

Leave the skins on the eggplants, but trim off and discard the stems and navels. Cut the eggplants in half lengthwise. Make slashes about 1 inch deep in their flesh on the cut sides and sprinkle them with salt. Place the halves cut sides down in a colander. Place the colander in the sink or over a dish and let stand so the bitter liquid drains out of the seeds, about 40 minutes.

Meanwhile, preheat an oven to 375 degrees F. Cover a baking sheet with aluminum foil.

Rinse the eggplant under cold water and pat dry thoroughly with a clean kitchen towel. In a small bowl, mix together the bread crumbs, oregano, parsley, the 1 tablespoon olive oil, and olives. Using your fingers, work as much of the mixture as you can into the slashes in the eggplant halves. Spread any remaining mixture on top of the eggplants. Place the eggplant halves cut sides up on the foil-lined sheet and drizzle generously with olive oil.

Bake on the middle rack of the oven until completely tender when pierced with a sharp knife, about 20 minutes. Serve hot, warm, or at room temperature.

*2 small eggplants (about ½ pound each)*

*salt for sprinkling on top of the eggplant*

*1 large clove garlic, finely chopped*

*2 tablespoons fine dried bread crumbs*

*1 teaspoon minced fresh oregano, or*
*½ teaspoon dried oregano*

*1 tablespoon chopped fresh Italian parsley*

*1 tablespoon extra-virgin olive oil, plus*
*additional olive oil for drizzling on*
*eggplants*

*1-½ tablespoons finely chopped, pitted*
*imported green olives*

# ZUCCHINE FARCITE ALLA LIGURE

❀

STUFFED ZUCCHINI, LIGURIA STYLE

FOR 4 PEOPLE

THE LIGURIANS ARE FAMOUS FOR THEIR STUFFED VEGETABLES. HERE IS A VERY TYPICAL WAY OF STUFFING ZUCCHINI AND MANY OTHER VEGETABLES.

4 young, tender zucchini
  (6 to 8 ounces each)
salt
¼ pound stale bread, crusts removed
⅓ cup milk
¼ pound fresh white cultivated
  mushrooms
3 tablespoons olive oil
2 large cloves garlic, finely chopped or
  passed through a garlic press
1 small onion, chopped
3 tablespoons chopped fresh Italian
  parsley
2 teaspoons chopped fresh marjoram, or
  1 teaspoon dried marjoram
1 egg, lightly beaten
freshly milled black pepper
7 tablespoons freshly grated parmigiano

Preheat an oven to 400 degrees F.

Wash the zucchini well to remove any imbedded dirt. Fill a large saucepan with water and bring to a boil. Add 1 tablespoon salt and the zucchini and boil until they are just tender but not too soft, about 10 minutes.

Meanwhile, shred the bread and place it in a small bowl with the milk to soak. Using a soft brush or clean kitchen towel, remove any dirt from the mushrooms. Trim off the tough bottoms from the stems and discard. Quarter the mushrooms and slice them thinly.

As soon as the zucchini are ready, drain them, or remove them from the steaming rack. When cool enough to handle, trim off their ends. Cut them in half lengthwise. With a paring knife, scoop out the flesh, leaving a shell about ¼ inch thick. Using your hands, wring out as much water as possible from the scooped out flesh. Chop it and set it aside.

Place the oil, garlic, and onion in a cold skillet over low heat. Sauté gently until the garlic and onion are softened but not colored, about 7 minutes. Add the parsley and sauté for an additional minute. Add the sliced mushrooms and marjoram to the skillet and sauté gently until the mushrooms are softened, about 8 minutes. Transfer to a bowl.

When the mushroom mixture has cooled, add the egg, salt (¾ teaspoon), pepper to taste, and 6 tablespoons of the *parmigiano*. Using your hands, squeeze out as much of the milk as possible from the bread. Add it and the chopped zucchini flesh to the bowl and mix thoroughly. Spoon the mixture into the zucchini shells, dividing it equally among them. Place the stuffed zucchini in a baking dish and sprinkle the remaining 1 tablespoon *parmigiano* over them.

Slip the dish onto the middle rack of the oven and bake until golden, about 30 minutes. Serve hot, warm, or at room temperature.

# POMODORI RIPIENI

✺

### STUFFED TOMATOES

THERE ARE MANY VERSIONS OF STUFFED TOMATOES, BOTH COOKED AND UNCOOKED. FILLING THE CAVITY WITH A STUFFING OF BREAD CRUMBS AND HERBS AND THEN BAKING THE TOMATOES IS A CLASSIC TREATMENT. THEY CAN BE SERVED AS A SIDE DISH, AS WELL AS AN **ANTIPASTO**. HOT VARIATIONS ON THE THEME OF STUFFED TOMATOES INCLUDE COOKING AN EGG INSIDE A BUTTERED TOMATO CAVITY; STUFFING THE CAVITY WITH A MIXTURE OF CHEESE AND SAFFRON-FLAVORED RICE OR A MIXTURE OF COOKED SPINACH AND CHEESE; AND STUFFING SMALL TOMATOES WITH SHREDDED MOZZARELLA. IN YET ANOTHER VARIATION, THE CAVITY IS FILLED WITH UNCOOKED RICE COMBINED WITH THE REMOVED TOMATO PULP AND SEASONINGS AND THEN BAKED. THESE ARE GOOD AS A MAIN COURSE AND CAN BE EATEN HOT OR AT ROOM TEMPERATURE. (IN ALL OF THESE RECIPES, THE "TOP" OF THE TOMATO IS REPLACED SO THAT THE FILLING COOKS PROPERLY.) ✺ COLD VEGETARIAN VARIATIONS INCLUDE FILLING THE CAVITY WITH A TASTY RICE SALAD SUCH AS THE ONE ON PAGE 34, OR WITH MAYONNAISE FLAVORED WITH HERBS AND CAPERS. BOTH OF THESE ARE EXCELLENT **ANTIPASTI** OR PICNIC OR BUFFET DISHES. ✺ IT IS NOT WORTH MAKING STUFFED TOMATOES UNLESS SWEET, FLAVORFUL, VINE-RIPENED TOMATOES ARE TO BE HAD, BUT THEY SHOULD BE QUITE FIRM IN ORDER TO FUNCTION SUCCESSFULLY AS A VESSEL FOR THE STUFFINGS.

## VERSIONE CALDA GRATINATA

✺

### HOT VERSION WITH BREAD CRUMBS AND HERBS

#### FOR 3 PEOPLE

Preheat an oven to 350 degrees F. Slice off the tops of the tomatoes and discard. Scrape out the seeds from the cavities, sprinkle the cavities lightly with salt, and then place the tomatoes upside down on a paper towel to drain for about 30 minutes.

Meanwhile, in a small bowl, combine the bread crumbs, garlic, herbs, olives (if using), ⅛ teaspoon salt, pepper to taste, and the 2 tablespoons olive oil. Spoon the mixture into the tomato cavities, dividing it evenly among them. Lightly oil a baking pan just about the right size to accommodate the tomatoes, so they will remain upright while they cook. Place the stuffed tomatoes in the

*3 firm vine-ripened tomatoes (about ¼ pound each)*

*salt*

*⅓ cup fine dried bread crumbs, lightly toasted (page 17)*

*1 large clove garlic, finely chopped or passed through a garlic press*

*2 teaspoons chopped fresh marjoram, or 1 teaspoon dried marjoram*

baking pan and drizzle lightly with more olive oil.

Bake until the tomatoes are golden brown, about 30 minutes. Serve warm or at room temperature.

2 tablespoons chopped fresh Italian
  parsley
1 tablespoon chopped fresh basil
  (optional)
3 tablespoons sliced pitted, sharp-flavored
  imported black olives (optional)
freshly milled black pepper
2 tablespoons extra-virgin olive oil, plus
  additional olive oil for oiling pan and
  for drizzling

## VERSIONE FREDDA CON MAIONESE ALLA LIGURE

❀

COLD VERSION WITH MAYONNAISE, LIGURIA STYLE

FOR 6 PEOPLE

WHILE AN EGG SALAD FILLING MIGHT SEEM MUNDANE, IT HAS A SPECIAL AFFINITY WITH TOMATOES. IN ANY CASE, THIS IS AN EGG SALAD IN THE ITALIAN FASHION—MADE WITH DELICIOUS HOMEMADE MAYONNAISE AND ZESTY CAPERS. SPRINKLE THE STUFFED TOMATOES WITH DRAINED SMALL CAPERS, IF YOU LIKE.

Slice off the tops of the tomatoes and discard. Scrape out the seeds from the cavities, sprinkle the cavities lightly with salt, and then place the tomatoes upside on a paper towel to drain for about 30 minutes.

Meanwhile, place the eggs in a saucepan with cold water to cover and bring to a boil. Reduce the heat to medium-low to prevent the eggs from knocking against each other as they cook. Cook for 7 minutes. Drain the eggs and run them under cold water. Immediately remove their shells. Allow them to cool somewhat.

Cut the eggs into small dice and place in a bowl. Add the mayonnaise and peppercorns or pepper and mix with a fork, tossing gently to coat. Spoon the mixture into the tomato cavities, dividing it equally among them. Serve immediately or refrigerate and serve within 3 hours.

4 firm vine-ripened tomatoes (about ¼
  pound each)
salt
2 extra-large eggs
3 tablespoons mayonnaise (page 29)
¼ teaspoon dried green peppercorns,
  crushed in a mortar, or a large pinch
  of freshly milled white or black pepper

# INSALATA CAPRESE

❋

## TANGY TOMATO AND MOZZARELLA SALAD, CAPRI STYLE

FOR 2 OR 3 PEOPLE

Tomatoes and mozzarella are a classic combination in southern Italian cooking, but they are especially compatible when raw. The tomatoes must be sweet, vine-ripened ones, however, and the mozzarella must be true mozzarella — that is, made the same day it is eaten and unrefrigerated (see pages 17–18 for information about mozzarella). The piquant, peppery dressing is a perfect foil for the blandness of the mozzarella, while the basil brings out the sweetness of the tomatoes and contributes contrasting color to the salad. Because refrigeration spoils the texture of fresh mozzarella and arrests the sweet taste of tomatoes, this salad should not be made more than an hour before it is to be served.

*3 tablespoons extra-virgin olive oil, plus additional olive oil for drizzling (optional)*

*1 teaspoon good red wine vinegar*

*large pinch red pepper flakes, or to taste*

*2 teaspoons drained small capers*

*¼ teaspoon chopped fresh oregano leaves, or ⅛ teaspoon dried oregano*

*4 small or 2 medium-sized sweet vine-ripened tomatoes*

*⅓ pound fresh mozzarella*

*6 fresh basil leaves*

In a small bowl, whisk together the 3 tablespoons oil, vinegar, pepper flakes, capers, and oregano. Cut the tomatoes into lengthwise slices. Cut the mozzarella into slices of about the same size.

Alternating the slices, arrange the tomatoes and mozzarella in an attractive manner on a serving plate. Pour the dressing over them, spooning the capers that remain on the bottom evenly on top. If desired, drizzle with additional olive oil. Tear the basil into pieces and scatter them over the salad. Serve at room temperature.

# POLENTA DI LODIGIANA

❋

CRISPY DEEP-FRIED POLENTA TOASTS, LOMBARDY STYLE

MAKES 14 POLENTA CROSTINI OR 7 POLENTA TRAMEZZINI

THESE LITTLE **CROSTINI**—ESSENTIALLY FRIED TOASTS—ARE IRRESISTIBLE **ANTIPASTI.** A VARIATION IS TO SLIP A THIN SLICE OF MOZZARELLA OR **FONTINA** IN BETWEEN TWO **POLENTA CROSTINI** BEFORE FRYING, THUS FORMING **TRAMEZZINI** (LITTLE SANDWICHES).

Lightly oil 2 large pastry boards or baking sheets, or a very large scratchproof counter surface. Make the *polenta* and, when it is cooked, turn it out onto the boards, counter top, or baking sheets. Using a large knife or rubber spatula dipped in water, spread the *polenta* out to a thickness of about ½ inch. Let it set until it is hardened, about 20 minutes.

Cut the cooled and hardened *polenta* into squares measuring approximately 3 inches. In a large skillet pour in olive oil to a depth of ½ inch. Heat the oil until it is hot enough to make a piece of hardened *polenta* sizzle instantly. Break the eggs into a shallow bowl and beat with a fork until blended. Place the bread crumbs in a separate shallow dish. If making *tramezzini*, cut the cheese into thin slices that are the exact shape of the *polenta* squares and slip a slice of cheese between 2 squares.

Just before you are ready to begin frying, dredge the *crostini* or *tramezzini* in flour. (As when frying any coated food, it is important not to cover the *polenta* squares with the coating until you are ready to fry them, or the coating will not be as crisp as it should be.) Dip them in the eggs, and then in the bread crumbs. Working in batches, slip the squares into the hot oil. Fry over medium heat on both sides, turning once, until golden brown, about 5 minutes on each side. They should be crispy when done; *tramezzini* should be crisp on the outside and the cheese filling completely melted. Fry only as many squares at a time as will fit without crowding the pan. Using a slotted spoon, remove to paper towels and drain briefly. Sprinkle with sea salt and serve piping hot.

AHEAD-OF-TIME NOTE: The *polenta* can be cooked, set, cut into squares or other shapes, well wrapped, and chilled for up to 3 days in advance of frying. Blot them with a paper towel before dredging and frying.

*olive oil for oiling work surface and for frying*
*½ recipe Basic Polenta (page 104)*
*3 extra-large eggs*
*all-purpose flour for dredging*
*about 1 cup fine dried bread crumbs, lightly toasted (page 17) for dredging*

*For the tramezzini:*
*½ pound mozzarella or fontina*
*sea salt*

# PEPERONATA

❀

SWEET PEPPER STEW

FOR 4 TO 6 PEOPLE

**T**HERE ARE MANY VERSIONS OF **PEPERONATA**. THE VENETIANS MIX IN EGGPLANT AND WHITE WINE. IN OTHER REGIONAL VARIATIONS, CAPERS ARE ADDED. I PREFER THIS, ONE OF THE SIMPLEST, BECAUSE I LOVE THE DIRECT, SIMPLE FLAVOR OF SWEET BELL PEPPERS WHEN THEY ARE STEWED WITH FEW OTHER DISTRACTING FLAVORS. WHILE RED PEPPERS ARE USUAL, I LIKE TO COMBINE RED AND YEL-LOW ONES BECAUSE THE TWO VIBRANT COLORS ARE STUNNING TOGETHER. **PEPERONATA** CAN BE SERVED AS AN **ANTIPASTO** WITH FRESH BREAD, **BRUSCHETTA**, OR **CROSTINI**, OR AS A SIDE DISH.

Cut the peppers in half lengthwise, derib them, and remove their stems and seeds. Slice them into long strips ½ inch wide. Set aside.

Warm the olive oil in a skillet over low heat. Add the onion and garlic and sauté gently until they are softened, 12 to 15 minutes. Add the pepper strips and sauté gently for 5 minutes, tossing. Add the tomatoes, cover, and cook gently, stirring occasionally, until the peppers are tender, 20 to 25 minutes.

Transfer to a serving dish and sprinkle with basil (if using). Serve hot, warm, or at room temperature.

AHEAD-OF-TIME NOTE: The flavor of *peperonata* is improved if it is made in advance and allowed to cool. It can be made 2 or even 3 days in advance of serv-ing, and even reheated if you prefer to serve it hot.

*6 medium-sized bell peppers, a mixture of red and yellow*

*5 tablespoons extra-virgin olive oil*

*1 large onion, quartered and finely sliced*

*4 cloves garlic, bruised*

*6 vine-ripened tomatoes, peeled, seeded, and chopped, or 1-½ cups canned plum tomatoes, drained, seeded, and chopped*

*6 large fresh basil leaves, torn into small pieces (optional)*

# BRUSCHETTA SEMPLICE

✦

TOASTED PEASANT BREAD WITH GARLIC AND OLIVE OIL

FOR 4 PEOPLE

**B**RUSCHETTA IS NOTHING MORE THAN THICK SLICES OF GOOD, STURDY PEASANT BREAD TOASTED OVER AN OPEN FIRE, RUBBED WITH FRESH GARLIC, THEN DRIZZLED WITH FRUITY OLIVE OIL. THIS IS A FAR CRY FROM WHAT AMERICANS HAVE COME TO KNOW AS GARLIC BREAD: BUTTER-SOAKED AIRY BREAD PERMEATED WITH ACRID GARLIC POWDER. **BRUSCHETTA**, ALSO CALLED **FETTUNTA** IN TUSCANY, IS SIMPLE ENOUGH AND HARDLY REQUIRES A RECIPE. BUT THERE ARE MANY VARIATIONS THAT MAKE DESCRIBING THE METHOD WORTHWHILE. ABOVE ALL, IT IS IMPORTANT TO USE GOOD ITALIAN-STYLE BREAD THAT IS STURDY, CHEWY, AND FLAVORFUL (PEASANT-STYLE LOAVES OR SEMOLINA OR EVEN SOURDOUGH BREADS ARE ACCEPTABLE) AND THE BEST EXTRA-VIRGIN OLIVE OIL.

*8 slices substantial bread, cut into slices*
*¼ inch thick*
*3 large cloves garlic, cut in half*
*lengthwise*
*⅓ cup extra-virgin olive oil*
*sea salt (optional)*

Just before serving, toast the bread lightly on both sides—preferably under a broiler or on a grill and not in a toaster. While still hot, rub each slice on one side with garlic, pressing to impregnate the bread with the juices from the garlic clove. Drizzle the garlic-rubbed side of each slice generously with olive oil. Sprinkle with salt, if desired, and serve.

BRUSCHETTA CON POMODORO E ERBE (VARIATION WITH TOMATO AND HERBS): Toast the bread lightly on both sides as directed in the basic *bruschetta* recipe. Meanwhile, in a small bowl combine ¼ cup extra-virgin olive oil; 1 large, sweet ripe tomato, seeded and chopped; ½ teaspoon finely chopped fresh thyme, or ¼ teaspoon crumbled dried thyme; 1 tablespoon finely chopped fresh basil; and salt and freshly milled black pepper to taste. While the toasted bread is still hot, rub it with the split garlic cloves as directed in the basic recipe. Spoon some of the mixture on each slice of bread. Serve immediately.

BRUSCHETTA UMBRA (VARIATION WITH LEMON, CAPERS, AND OLIVES, UMBRIA STYLE): Toast the bread lightly on both sides as directed in the basic *bruschetta* recipe. Meanwhile, in a small bowl stir together ¼ cup extra-virgin olive oil, 1 tablespoon freshly squeezed lemon juice, 3 tablespoons chopped, pitted imported green olives, and 2 teaspoons drained small capers. While the toasted bread is still hot, rub it with split garlic cloves as directed in the basic recipe. Spoon some of the mixture on each slice of bread. Serve immediately.

# VERDURA FRITTA

�֍

### BATTER-FRIED VEGETABLES

THESE ARE ONLY TWO OF THE MANY **PASTELLE** ("BATTERS") ONE FINDS IN ITALIAN COOKING. OTHERS MAY CONTAIN EGGS OR BEATEN EGG WHITES, OR, WINE. THE FIRST OF THESE TWO BATTERS FORMS A STICKY COATING ON FOODS THAT PREVENTS THE FRYING OIL FROM PENETRATING, THUS GIVING LIGHT, CRISP RESULTS. THE SECOND BATTER, MADE WITH YEAST, FORMS A PUFFIER COATING. A VARIATION ON THE BATTER-DIPPED FRITTER THEME ARE THE SCRUMPTIOUS, CRUNCHY FRITTERS IN CHAPTER 5, **CONTORNI E INSALATE**, WHICH HAVE AN EGG-AND-BREAD-CRUMB COATING. BATTER-FRIED VEGETABLES CAN ALSO BE SERVED AS SIDE DISHES, BUT I ALWAYS PREFER TO PUT THEM IN A CATEGORY OF THEIR OWN; IN THIS CASE, BEFORE THE MEAL, WHERE THEY ENTICE RATHER THAN COMPETE WITH OTHER DISHES. �֍ THE MOST IMPORTANT THING TO REMEMBER WHEN PREPARING FOODS FOR BATTER-FRYING IS TO DRY THEM THOROUGHLY BEFORE SLIPPING THEM INTO THE BATTER. TO INSURE A CRISPY COATING, COAT THE VEGETABLES THINLY WITH THE BATTER, LETTING THE EXCESS DROP BACK INTO THE BOWL. AND, OF COURSE, THE OIL MUST BE HOT ENOUGH TO MAKE THE COATED FOODS SIZZLE UPON CONTACT AND THE PAN MUST NOT BE CROWDED WITH FOODS OR THE OIL TEMPERATURE WILL DROP. AFTER FRYING, LIFT OUT THE FOODS WITH A SLOTTED SPOON AND DRAIN WELL ON BOTH SIDES. DON'T STACK FRIED FOODS IN LAYERS TO DRAIN OR THEY WILL BECOME SOGGY. INSTEAD, PLACE THEM ON A LARGE PLATTER, LINED WITH PAPER TOWELS, IN A SINGLE LAYER.

---

*1 cup water*

*freshly milled white pepper (omit if frying fruits)*

*⅔ cup all-purpose flour*

*1 package active dry yeast*

*½ teaspoon sugar*

*1-¼ cups warm water*

*½ teaspoon salt*

*freshly milled white pepper (omit if frying fruits)*

*1-½ cups all purpose flour*

METHOD 1 Makes enough batter for 1 pound prepared vegetables or fruits.

Put the water and pepper to taste in a bowl. Sift in the flour and, using a fork or a whisk, beat to make a smooth, creamy mixture. Cover the bowl and allow the batter to stand at room temperature for 2 to 3 hours. Use immediately or refrigerate for up to 3 days.

METHOD 2 Makes enough batter for 2 pounds prepared vegetables or fruits.

Put the yeast into a bowl. Add the sugar and ¼ cup of the warm water. Allow to stand until the yeast is creamy, about 10 minutes. Add the remaining 1 cup warm water, salt, and pepper to taste, then sift in the flour. Using a fork or whisk, beat the mixture well until smooth and light. Cover the bowl and set it in a warm place until the batter is doubled, about 2 hours.

Stir and use immediately, or cover and refrigerate for up to 24 hours. When refrigerated overnight, the batter will separate. Use a fork or whisk to return it to a uniform mixture before using it.

# INSALATE COMPOSTE

❈

## SALADS OF COOKED VEGETABLES

**B**OTH OF THESE SALADS ARE TYPICAL TREATMENTS OF VEGETABLES IN THE ITALIAN KITCHEN, AND BOTH ARE USUALLY SERVED AS **ANTIPASTI** RATHER THAN AS **CONTORNI.**

METHOD 1 There is hardly a simpler way to prepare cooked vegetables than this one: Boil vegetables such as beets, green beans, or asparagus until tender and then sprinkle with good fruity olive oil. It is best to anoint the cooked vegetables with the olive oil while they are still warm because the heat releases the scent and flavor of the oil. Fresh lemon should be added only at the moment of eating, because it discolors certain vegetables (in particular, broccoli and green beans) soon after contact. A delightful salad can also be made of various boiled vegetables mixed together. In addition to the vegetables mentioned above, you might add cauliflower, carrots, fresh artichoke hearts, and zucchini to an *insalata composta.*

I have found that American red beets leach their color into the other vegetables when added to these salads, so I prefer to serve them on their own, boiled, peeled, sliced, and dressed with extra-virgin olive oil and vinegar instead of lemon. Yellow beets are sometimes found in farmer's markets; they are preferable to red beets for *insalate composte.*

METHOD 2 Another variety of cooked vegetable salad is what in Liguria is called *giardiniera,* or what in Piedmont is called *insalata russa.* It is a salad of diced boiled vegetables dressed with homemade mayonnaise. Boil green beans, beets, carrots, potatoes, peas, and zucchini separately in salted water until they are tender but firm; drain and cut into small pieces. In a serving bowl, toss the vegetables together with a little olive oil, and then dress them with homemade mayonnaise (the lemony mayonnaise on page 29 is ideal). Cauliflower and onions should not be included in *insalata russa.*

# SOTT'ACETI

✸

## PICKLED VEGETABLES

MAKES 1 QUART PICKLED VEGETABLES

OTHER VEGETABLES SUCH AS CELERY AND ZUCCHINI MAY BE INCLUDED FOR **SOTT'ACETI** (LITER-ALLY, "UNDER VINEGAR"). FRESH FENNEL IS ESPECIALLY GOOD PREPARED THIS WAY BECAUSE ITS NATURAL SWEETNESS IS A FOIL FOR THE ACIDITY OF THE VINEGAR. **SOTT'ACETI** ARE USUALLY SERVED WITH OTHER **ANTIPASTI** DISHES, OR, ON THE NONVEGETARIAN TABLE, WITH COLD MEATS.

*For the marinade:*

*3 cups good-quality white wine vinegar*

*2 cups water*

*¼ cup extra-virgin olive oil*

*5 tablespoons sugar*

*2 teaspoons salt*

*12 allspice berries*

*20 whole cloves*

*2 large bay leaves*

*2 bulbs fennel*

*½ pound baby carrots, scraped, or 3 medium-sized carrots, scraped and sliced on the diagonal*

*¼ pound pearl onions*

*½ small cauliflower, divided into small florets*

*4 large cloves garlic, bruised*

*4 small dried hot red peppers*

*1 red bell pepper, seeded, deribbed, and cut into strips*

*1 yellow bell pepper, seeded, deribbed, and cut into strips*

*extra-virgin olive oil for serving*

In a nonaluminum pot, combine all the ingredients for the marinade and bring to a boil. Reduce the heat to low and simmer for 10 minutes. Meanwhile, cut off the stalks and fronds from the fennel bulbs. Cut a slice off the tough base of each. Trim off any brown spots. Cut each bulb lengthwise into 8 wedges.

When the marinade has simmered for 10 minutes, add the fennel, carrots, onions, cauliflower, garlic, and hot peppers. Cover and bring to a boil; immediately remove the cover, add the bell peppers, lower the heat to medium, and simmer, uncovered, for 2 minutes. Using a slotted spoon, immediately remove all the vegetables from the liquid and set them aside in a bowl to cool. Cool the liquid completely.

When both the vegetables and the liquid (do not strain) have cooled, reunite them in an attractive glass jar. Cover the jar and refrigerate for 3 days to a week before serving.

The vegetables are best eaten within 2 weeks, but they will keep for about 3 weeks. Keep in mind that the longer they soak in the marinade, the more pungent their flavor will be. Store them in the refrigerator. Sprinkle the vegetables with extra-virgin olive oil before serving.

# MELANZANE SOTT'ACETO ALL'AMENDOLARA

❀

ANNA AMENDOLARA'S PICKLED EGGPLANT

MAKES 6 PINTS

U SE SMALL EGGPLANTS FOR THIS RECIPE; THEY ARE MILDER AND CONTAIN FEWER SEEDS THAN LARGER ONES.

Peel the eggplants. Cut them into strips ¼ inch thick and ¼ inch wide. Place the eggplant strips in a nonreactive (plastic or stainless-steel) colander and toss them with 1-½ tablespoons of the salt. Place a plate on the eggplant and top the plate with a weight. Place the colander in the sink and let stand so the bitter liquid drains out of the seeds, 30 to 40 minutes.

Rinse the eggplant quickly under cold running water. Then, working with a handful at a time, squeeze out all the excess water from it.

In a saucepan bring the vinegar, water, red pepper flakes, and sugar to a boil. Add the eggplant. Over the highest heat possible, cook the eggplant for 2 minutes. With a skimmer or slotted spoon, lift the eggplant out and transfer it to a nonreactive bowl. Reserve the vinegar marinade.

Wash six 1-pint mason jars in hot, soapy water, rinse well, and invert them on a clean cloth towel to drain. Bring a large pan of water to a boil and immerse the jars in the water, one at a time. Remove the jar with tongs, drain well, and, while the jar is still hot, fill it halfway with some of the eggplant. Add 4 teaspoons of the capers (if using), ½ teaspoon of the oregano, and 1 of the sliced garlic cloves. Fill the jar with more eggplant to within 1 inch of the top. Repeat this procedure with the remaining jars and ingredients. Return the vinegar marinade to the heat and bring it to a boil. Ladle it into the jars, filling them to within ½ inch of the top. Wipe the rims of the jars with a clean, damp cloth. Immerse the lids in boiling water and cover the jars. Screw on the rings and let stand until completely cool. Check the lids for a good seal; they should be slightly concave and not push back when pressed. Label, date, and store the jars in a cool, dark place.

To serve the pickled eggplant, drain it and toss with extra-virgin olive oil.

*6 pounds small eggplants*
*2-½ tablespoons salt*
*6 cups distilled white vinegar*
*2 cups water*
*2 teaspoons red pepper flakes*
*1-½ tablespoons sugar*
*½ cup drained small capers*
  *(optional)*
*1 tablespoon dried oregano*
*6 cloves garlic, sliced lengthwise*
*extra-virgin olive oil for serving*

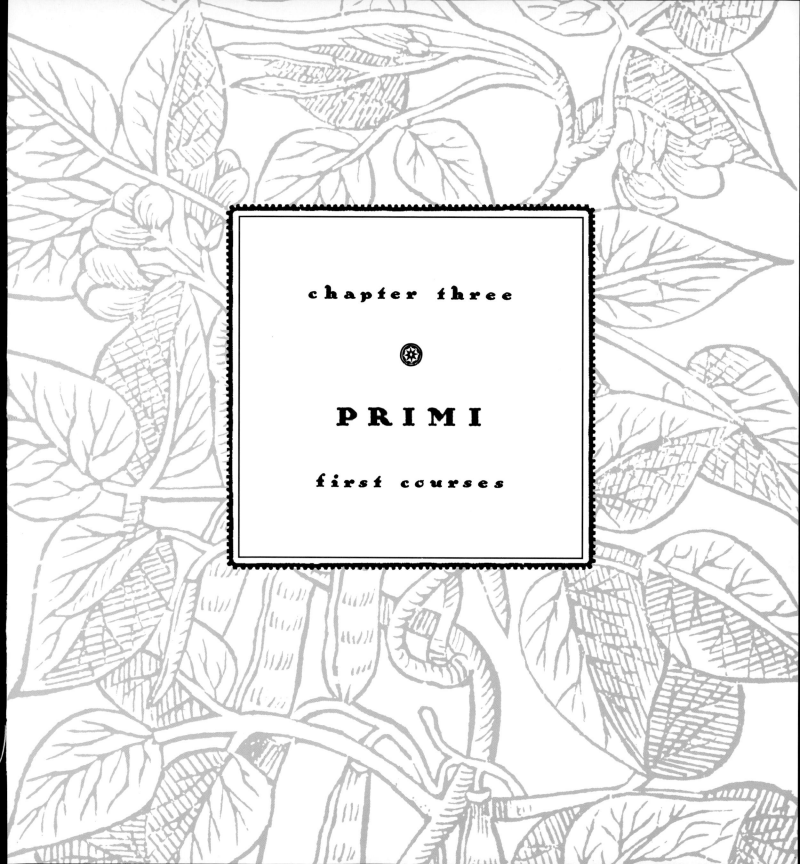

chapter three

PRIMI

first courses

I N ITALY, THE **PRIMO**, OR FIRST COURSE, IS USUALLY THE MOST SUBSTANTIAL ELEMENT OF THE MEAL. THIS COURSE IS ALSO CALLED THE **MINESTRA**, WHICH MEANS SIMPLY "SOUP." To avoid confusion, I refer here to first courses as *primi piatti*, or *primi*. There are two types of *primi*, those that are *in brodo*, or wet (literally, "in broth"), and those that are *asciutta*, that is, "dry." In the first category are included *minestrine*, light soups; *minestre*, thicker vegetable soups or purées; *minestroni*, vegetable and pasta or grain soups; and *zuppe*, hearty, thick soups that often include bread. Cream is never added to soup in the Italian kitchen. In the *asciutta* grouping are included fresh and dried pasta dishes, *gnocchi* (dumplings), and *risotti*. In Italy, soups are never served in the same meal with other *primi* such as pasta or *risotto*.

When most Americans think of Italian vegetarian soups, they probably think of the "minestrone" of American-Italian restaurants, which is almost always a standard vegetable soup with pasta and beans in it. In fact, there are infinite variations on the theme of *minestrone*, literally, "big soup." Americans are not to be faulted for this. Italian immigrants imported to America relatively few of the dishes of which Italy's amazingly varied cuisine is comprised. After all, the immigrants from the *mezzogiorno*, as the poor Italian south is known, came here because they had nothing to eat. They had, in essence, become disenfranchised from their culinary culture as a result of their poverty.

There are numerous reasons for the wonderful variety of soups found in Italy. The traditional Italian housewife, rich or poor, looked to heaven as well as into her purse when contemplating what to put on the dinner table. On Fridays, the Catholic religion forbade the consumption of animal flesh, and therefore a meatless menu had to be devised. With typical panache, these inventive cooks created a whole world of quick, healthful, and delectable *zuppe di magro*, or "lean soups." Casting about for ingredients, they naturally looked to vegetables and other inexpensive staples.

Pasta has long been the staff of life in many parts of Italy, and beans have been an equally ubiquitous element of the *cucina povera*. Pasta and beans inevitably found themselves *senza* meat in the soup pot, and *pasta e fagioli* became an Italian classic. This happy marriage of pasta and beans takes on infinite variety throughout each of Italy's nineteen regions. As with so many Italian dishes, the variations reflect the lay of the land—mountains, coastlines, and valleys. Climate and temperament as well as history and custom are also mirrored in the colors and compositions of these peasant dishes. Thus this chapter contains numerous regional variations of *pasta e fagioli* as well as other soups. In remote Sardinia, for example, *pasta e fagioli* sometimes takes the form of a soup of chick-peas, wild fennel, and *fregula*, an Arab-inspired couscouslike pasta unique to the island. (I substitute *ditalini* here, because *fregula* is unavailable.) In this land of sheepherders, slivers of *pecorino* are a common addition. In raucous Rome and its environs, on the other hand, a teeming assembly of a seemingly impossible number of vegetables, pasta, and beans unite in a soup that only such a vegetable-loving people could devise. Meanwhile, in vastly poor Apulia, a meatless lentil soup is made thick and hearty with the addition of spaghetti.

The more delicate *minestrine*, literally, "little soups," are altogether different in character. First of all, of fundamental importance is the flavor of the broth on which these soups are based. There is no reason why light vegetarian soups should be insipid. I have experimented with many vegetable broths, and have developed one that is packed with good vegetable flavor (page 58). This broth is the basis of many of the soups and *risotti* in this book. *Minestrine* are not meant to be crowded with vegetables, rice, pasta, and such. If fine soup pasta (*pastina*) or rice is added to it, their proportion should be small so that the broth can be appreciated fully. Indeed, the broth is so tasty it is delicious on its own. Broths might also contain *tortellini* or other small stuffed pasta or dumplings. In Trentino–Alto Adige, very thin *crêpes* of egg, flour, milk, and parsley are cut into thin ribbons and served in broth in a dish called *frittatensuppe*.

Italians use other devices besides tasty broth to add flavor to nonmeat soups. In Liguria, *pesto*, the heady, aromatic basil, pine nut, and *parmigiano* paste for which that region is famous, is almost always added to *minestrone* at the table. Grated cheese, either *parmigiano* or *pecorino*, added to many soups at the table, is a tremendous flavor boost. Extra-virgin olive oil is another flavor enhancer when drizzled into soups that have enough body to support it, such as thick vegetable soups or pasta-and-bean soups. In the absence of a flavorful vegetable broth, good-quality bouillon cubes can also intensify flavor when crushed into a *soffritto* that is the basis of a soup or *risotto*. One should be careful in purchasing such cubes, however, because most brands contain monosodium glutamate and other artificial substances heretical in good cooking.

As well as economy and religion, resourcefulness and creativity are at the heart of the tremendous diversity of vegetarian soups. Who would ever think, for example, that soup could be made from bread? In Sardinia, slices of stale bread are layered in a casserole with tangy fresh *pecorino* and local herbs, then steeped in broth and baked. While the dish is called a *zuppa*, it resembles a cake when it comes out of the oven. In Florence, *pappa al pomodoro* is a local specialty. This delicious soup is made from nothing more than stale bread, sweet fresh tomatoes, basil, water or broth, and fruity olive oil. There are numerous others: the *acquacotta* (literally, "cooked water") of Maremma, onion, celery, tomato, and olive oil cooked together and topped with toasted bread and sometimes cheese; the Tuscan *zuppa di pane*, a thick soup of vegetables, beans, and stale bread; and the famous *ribollita* ("reboiled"), a similar soup that is literally cooked twice.

Pasta, fresh or dry, is a delicious medium for vegetables and vegetarian sauces. My two previous books discuss in great detail the differences between dried and fresh pasta, the making of fresh pasta, and the proper mating of pasta shapes and varieties to sauces. The pasta recipes in this chapter reflect regional differences as well as a variety of cooking styles, from delicate to hearty.

There are many ways of cooking rice in the Italian kitchen. But the most common is *risotto*, a uniquely Italian method. The rice is first sautéed in butter, then cooked gradually with small amounts of broth added to it until the kernels fully absorb the liquid. The resulting texture is very creamy. (The Venetians like their *risotto all'onda*, "with a wave"; in other words, they prefer it soupy, which is not surprising for a people surrounded by water.) Classic *risotto* is made with homemade meat or fish broth. But the full-bodied vegetable broth I use makes a marvelous *risotto*. Just as with pasta, the possibilities for *risotto* are endless. They are a perfect vehicle for almost any vegetable, from artichokes to *radicchio*, from mushrooms to pumpkins. They can also be based on cheese(s) or wine, or prepared very simply with nothing more than *odori*, aromatic vegetables such as onion, and butter.

It should be pointed out that while traditionally *primi* are meant to be followed by the second course of meat, fish, or fowl, many pasta, rice, and even soup dishes are substantial enough to satisfy modern people for a main course.

# BRODO VEGETALE

❋

VEGETABLE BROTH

MAKES ABOUT 8 CUPS (2 QUARTS)

VEGETABLE BROTHS CAN BE INSIPID, BUT THIS VEGETABLE BROTH I MAKE IS VERY FLAVORFUL BECAUSE THE VEGETABLES ARE FIRST SAUTEÉD IN BUTTER. BE CAREFUL, HOWEVER, NOT TO BROWN THE VEGETABLES, OR THE BROTH WILL LOSE ITS DELICACY AND PLEASANT COLOR. THE VEGETABLES NEED NOT BE DISCARDED AFTER THE STOCK IS COOKED; THEY CAN BE CHOPPED OR PURÉED AND ADDED TO THE BROTH IF IT IS TO BE EATEN AS A SOUP. THE BROTH ALONE CAN BE EATEN AS A CONSOMMÉ. FOR AN INTENSELY FLAVOR-PACKED BROTH, REDUCE THE QUANTITY OF WATER BY A CUP OR TWO. IT IS VERY USEFUL TO HAVE THIS BROTH ON HAND OR STORED IN THE FREEZER BECAUSE IT IS THE FOUNDATION OF SO MANY VEGETARIAN (AND OTHER) DISHES.

*1 large leek*

*3 tablespoons unsalted butter*

*3 carrots, scraped and sliced*

*2 onions, diced*

*2 large celery stalks, diced, plus a handful of coarsely chopped celery leaves*

*4 small or 2 large bay leaves*

*8 cups (2 quarts) water*

*1 teaspoon black peppercorns*

*a handful of parsley, leaves and stems*

*1 tablespoon salt, or to taste*

Trim off the roots and discolored parts of the stem of the leek and discard them. Slice it in half lengthwise and spread open the sheaths under cold running water to wash out any sand that is lodged between them. Slice thinly crosswise.

In a large soup kettle over medium-low heat, melt the butter. Add the leek, carrots, onions, celery stalks and leaves, and bay leaves. Sauté the vegetables gently without letting them brown, about 10 minutes. Add 1 cup of the water, stir, and cover. Cook gently for an additional 20 minutes, stirring occasionally.

Remove the cover, add the remaining 7 cups water, the peppercorns, and parsley. Re-cover and cook over low heat for 1-½ hours. Season with the salt.

To eat the broth on its own, strain it and remove and discard the bay leaves, peppercorns, and parsley stalks. Chop or purée the vegetables and return them to the broth. If using the broth in recipes calling for vegetable broth, strain the stock through a sieve, pressing on the vegetables with the back of a large wooden spoon to extract as much of the flavor from the vegetables as possible. Use as directed in the recipe.

AHEAD-OF-TIME NOTE: This broth can be made 2 or 3 days in advance of using, cooled, covered, and refrigerated. Or it may be frozen for up to 3 months.

ZUPPA CASALINGA (HOUSEWIFE'S SOUP): This is one of my favorite quick dishes based on this broth. For 2 people, take 4 slices (about ¼ pound) flavorful, sturdy Italian bread that has gone stale and arrange them on the bottom of an ovenproof casserole. Top the bread with 2 ounces thinly sliced *fontina*, then sprinkle with ¼ cup freshly grated *parmigiano*. Ladle 2 cups of the hot broth over the bread and cheese and bake in a preheated 375 degree F oven until bubbly, about 20 minutes. To serve more people, more bread topped with the cheeses can be layered in the casserole and proportionately greater quantitites of hot broth ladled over the layers.

MINESTRA DI FARRO ALLA SARDA (BROTH WITH SPELT, SHEEP'S CHEESE, AND MINT, SARDINIA STYLE): *Farro*, called spelt in English, is an ancient grain that is still used in the regional cuisines of Sardinia, Latium, and Liguria. This nourishing, chewy, nutty grain, found in many natural-food stores, resembles unhulled rice or barley. In Sardinia, *farro* is cooked in broth, then fresh *pecorino*, soft sheep's milk cheese aged no longer than 1 week, and chopped fresh mint are sprinkled on top before serving. While meat broth is traditional, this tasty vegetable broth can be substituted. For *minestra di farro*, soak 1 cup *farro* overnight in cold water to cover. Drain. Bring the vegetable broth to a boil. Add the *farro*, cover, and cook gently until the *farro* is tender, 45 to 50 minutes. Ladle into individual soup bowls. Top with slices (about ½ pound total) of young, mild *pecorino*, *fior di Sardegna*, Tuscan *caciotta*, or semisoft goat's milk cheese. Sprinkle with chopped fresh mint. Eat piping hot.

PASSATO DI VERDURA ALLA ZIETTA NELLA (MY AUNT NELLA'S PURÉE OF VEGETABLE SOUP): Years after my *zia* Nella made a facsimile of this soup for our family when we visited her in Rome, I thought about its lovely flavor. I tried many different puréed vegetable soups hoping to recapture it. When I finally asked her about it recently, she listed the predictable ingredi-ents—carrots, celery, leeks, potatoes, and parsley—and *rapa*, or "turnip." Large yellow turnips, properly called rutabagas, are preferable because they have a stronger flavor than the smaller white variety tinged with purple. But either or both varieties can be used. Follow the directions for vegetable broth, but add 1 large (about ¾ pound) potato, peeled and diced, and ¾ pound rutabagas or turnips, also peeled and diced, to the pot along with the cup of water after the other vegetables have been sautéed. Add an additional ½ cup water at the same time. When the soup is finished cooking, allow it to cool somewhat, then pass it through a food mill to purée it. Return the puréed soup to the pot to heat through and add more salt to taste. Serve hot.

# MINESTRONE ROMANO "A CRUDO"

❊

## "RAW" MINESTRONE, ROMAN STYLE

### FOR 8 TO 10 PEOPLE

THE SECRET TO THE SUCCESS OF THIS SPECTACULARLY COLORFUL VEGETABLE SOUP IS THE USE OF UNCOMPROMISINGLY FRESH VEGETABLES, GOOD QUALITY, EXTRA-VIRGIN OLIVE OIL, AND AUTHENTIC **PARMIGIANO-REGGIANO** CHEESE. **A CRUDO** REFERS TO THE FACT THAT THE VEGETABLES ARE RAW WHEN THEY ARE PUT INTO THE BROTH RATHER THAN BEING ADDED TO A **SOFFRITTO** BASE (A SAUTÉED MIXTURE OF OIL, ONION OR GARLIC, AND PARSLEY), WHICH IS OFTEN PREPARED AS A MEANS OF HEIGHTENING THE FLAVORS OF THE VEGETABLES BEFORE THEY ARE COMBINED WITH WATER OR BROTH. IF THE VEGETABLES ARE VERY FRESH, HOWEVER, THIS STEP IS UNNECESSARY. A **BATTUTO** (CHOPPED MIXTURE) OF GARLIC, ROSEMARY, AND PARSLEY ADDED AT THE LAST MINUTE LENDS EXTRA FLAVOR TO THIS STRICTLY VEGETARIAN SOUP. ANOTHER METHOD FOR GIVING A BOOST OF FLAVOR IS THE LIGURIAN ONE OF STIRRING A FEW TABLESPOONS OF **PESTO** (PAGE 74) INTO THE SOUP JUST BEFORE SERVING.

*3 tablespoons extra-virgin olive oil, plus additional olive oil for the table*

*3 canned plum tomatoes, seeded and chopped, plus ¼ cup of their juices*

*1 large onion, chopped coarsely*

*1 potato, peeled and diced*

*1 large celery stalk, thinly sliced, plus the leaves, chopped*

*¾ pound butternut squash, diced (1-½ cups)*

*2 teaspoons fresh rosemary, or 1 teaspoon dried rosemary, plus 3 tablespoons chopped fresh rosemary, or 2 tablespoons dried rosemary*

*3 tablespoons finely chopped fresh Italian parsley leaves and stems, plus 3 tablespoons chopped fresh Italian parsley*

In a large pot, combine the 3 tablespoons oil, the tomatoes and juice, onion, potato, celery and leaves, squash, the 2 teaspoons rosemary, the 3 tablespoons finely chopped parsley, the carrot, cabbage, cranberry beans (reserve canned beans, if using), water, salt, and pepper. Cover the pot and bring to a boil over high heat. Immediately reduce the heat to medium-low, cover with the lid askew, and simmer for about 40 minutes, or until the cranberry beans are cooked.

Add the green beans, zucchini, cauliflower, and pasta; cook for 8 minutes. Stir in the garlic, the 3 tablespoons rosemary, and the 3 tablespoons chopped parsley; if using canned beans, add them at this point. Continue cooking the soup, uncovered, over medium heat, until the pasta is not quite *al dente* (it will not remain so, since it soaks in the hot soup, so it is best to undercook it somewhat), about 8 minutes.

Serve the soup with abundant freshly grated *parmigiano*, a dribble of olive oil, and pepper to taste.

There are infinite variations on the theme of *minestrone* which means, literally, "big soup." These reflect regional cooking style as well as availability of ingredients. In summer almost any vegetable in season might be used in *minestrone*. This would include other summer squash varieties, swiss chard, fresh peas, fresh fava

beans, carrots and celery. In winter, cabbage, many varieties of dried beans and other cold weather vegetables predominate.

In the non vegetarian version of this soup a large meaty ham bone or ham hock are typically included.

NOTE: If you like, 1 cup dried *cannellini* beans can be substituted for the fresh cranberry beans or canned beans. To rehydrate and cook them, see page 15.

1 large carrot, scraped and diced

½ pound green cabbage, finely shredded (about 1-½ cups)

1 pound fresh cranberry beans, shelled (1 to 1-½ cups shelled), or 2 cups drained canned pinto or pink beans, rinsed and drained (see note for dried beans)

3 quarts (12 cups) water

2 tablespoons salt, or to taste

plenty of freshly milled black pepper

¼ pound green beans, cut into 1-inch lengths (about 1 cup)

2 small zucchini, cut crosswise into slices ½ inch thick

1-½ cups cauliflower florets

1 cup conchigliette ("little shells") or ditalini ("little thimbles") pasta

4 large cloves garlic, finely chopped

freshly grated parmigiano

# PAPPA AL POMODORO

❋

## FLORENTINE TOMATO AND BREAD SOUP

FOR 4 PEOPLE

ONE OF ITALY'S MOST HUMBLE SOUPS, **PAPPA AL POMODORO** (**PAPPA** MEANS "PAP," SOMETHING SOFT) IS SO SIMPLE TO MAKE AND SO GOOD THAT ANYONE WITH TOMATOES IN THE GARDEN WILL WANT TO TRY IT. THE AMOUNT OF WATER NECESSARY WILL DEPEND UPON HOW MUCH THE BREAD ABSORBS. THERE ARE MANY VERSIONS OF THIS SOUP. IN SOME, THE SOUP IS COOKED FOR A LONG TIME, EVEN FOR AS LONG AS AN HOUR. I LIKE TO MINIMIZE THE COOKING TIME IN ORDER TO PRESERVE THE CLEAR, FRESH TOMATO TASTE.

In a saucepan, bring to boil enough water to cover the tomatoes. Plunge the tomatoes into the boiling water for 30 seconds. Remove them promptly and place them under cold running water. Using a paring knife, peel off the skins. Cut the tomatoes in half and remove the seeds; dice the tomatoes.

In a saucepan over medium-high heat, warm the ¼ cup oil and garlic together. Sauté gently until the garlic is lightly golden, about 4 minutes. Add the tomatoes and about 2 tablespoons of the basil. Simmer over medium-low heat until the tomatoes thicken, about 20 minutes. Add the broth and bring to a boil. Add the bread and toss all the ingredients together. Continue to cook just until heated through and the bread absorbs the liquid completely. Remove the garlic cloves (don't throw them away, as they can be spread onto bread). Add the salt and pepper to taste.

Ladle into individual serving bowls. Divide the remaining 1 tablespoon or so of basil among the bowls, sprinkling it on top, and drizzle with additional olive oil.

*2-¼ pounds (4 large) ripe, vine-ripened tomatoes*

*¼ cup extra-virgin olive oil, plus additional olive oil for drizzling*

*4 large cloves garlic, bruised*

*a handful of fresh basil leaves, torn into small pieces (about 3 tablespoons)*

*about 4 cups Vegetable Broth (page 58) or water*

*½ pound stale bread, still soft enough to be torn, shredded*

*1-¼ teaspoons salt*

*freshly milled black or white pepper*

# ZUPPA GALLURESE VEGETALE

❀

## SAVORY BREAD AND CHEESE SOUP FROM GALLURA

### FOR 6 TO 8 PEOPLE

IT IS HARD TO KNOW WHAT TO CALL THIS DISH, FOR IT IS MORE A CASSEROLE OR SAVORY CAKE THAN A SOUP. IT IS INSPIRED BY A SARDINIAN DISH CALLED **ZUPPA GALLURESE**, "SOUP FROM GALLURA," A QUIDDITY OF THE PROVINCE OF GALLURA. AS THE SARDINIAN WRITER MARLENA CANNAS EXPLAINS IN **LA CUCINA DEI SARDI**, THE DISH REFLECTS TOTALLY THE SHEPHERD'S LIFE AND, THEREFORE, THE CULTURE OF GALLURA. IN THE ORIGINAL DISH, THE THREE MAIN INGREDIENTS ARE THE SHEPHERD'S STAPLES: BREAD, MEAT (BROTH IN THIS CASE), AND SHEEP'S CHEESE. I HAVE MADE IT SUCCESSFULLY WITH THE FULL-BODIED VEGETABLE BROTH ON PAGE 58 (THE AMOUNT NEEDED WILL DEPEND UPON HOW HARD THE BREAD IS). ❀ THIS BREAD SOUP IS EASY TO REPRODUCE IN AMERICAN KITCHENS, AS LONG AS GOOD, STURDY BREAD IS AVAILABLE (SEMOLINA OR SOURDOUGH BREAD IS PARTICULARLY SUITABLE). SHEEP'S CHEESE (**PECORINO**), BOTH SOFT AND HARD, CAN BE FOUND IN AMERICAN MARKETS, SO DON'T BE TEMPTED TO SUBSTITUTE MOZZARELLA, WHICH IS FAR TOO BLAND AND OOZY FOR THIS PURPOSE. FRESH SHEEP'S MILK CHEESE IS NOT SO COMMON AS AGED **PECORINO** IN AMERICAN MARKETS, BUT FRESH (SOFT) GOAT'S CHEESE CAN BE SUBSTITUTED. A GOOD AGED **PROVOLONE** COULD BE A SUBSTITUTE FOR AGED **PECORINO**; IT SHOULD NOT BE THE INNOCUOUS DOMESTIC VARIETY, HOWEVER. THIS DISH, WHICH IS MORE LIKE A PUDDING THAN A SOUP, CAN INDEED BE SUPPER IF ACCOMPANIED WITH VEGETABLES. FOR THE NONVEGETARIAN, IT MAKES A LOVELY SIDE DISH FOR A ROAST OF ANY KIND. ❀ I HAVE INCLUDED TWO VARIATIONS, ONE WITH FRESH FENNEL AND ONE WITH SUN-DRIED TOMATOES, BOTH TYPICAL SARDINIAN VARIATIONS. ALL THREE VERSIONS ARE MARVELOUS EXAMPLES OF HOW EXCEPTIONALLY GOOD THE FOOD OF ITALIAN PEASANTS CAN BE. ONCE YOU BEGIN TO MAKE THIS WONDERFUL "SOUP," YOU WILL NO DOUBT CREATE MANY OF YOUR OWN VARIATIONS.

*Extra-virgin olive oil for oiling dish,*
*plus ¼ cup extra-virgin olive oil*
*1-¼ pounds stale bread, still soft*
*enough to cut*
*6 ounces fresh (soft) sheep's milk or*
*goat's milk cheese, sliced*
*½ cup freshly grated aged* pecorino

Preheat an oven to 350 degrees F. Select a 10-by-14-inch (or equivalent-sized) baking dish (preferably nonstick) with high sides. Brush it generously with extra-virgin olive oil.

Trim the crusts from the bread and discard; cut the bread into thin slices. Using one third of the bread, form a layer of the bread on the bottom of the prepared dish. Arrange half of the soft cheese over the bread. Top with a layer of half of the grated hard cheese. Mix together the rosemary and thyme and sprinkle half of it over the cheese. Drizzle with one third of the ¼ cup olive oil.

Repeat the layers with the remaining ingredients, ending with a layer of bread and using about half of the remaining oil. Pour the broth over the mixture, then drizzle with the remaining olive oil. Cover the baking dish tightly with a lid or aluminum foil.

Place on the center rack of the oven and bake until the *zuppa* is set, bubbling, and golden, 50 to 60 minutes. Remove it from the oven and allow it to settle for 5 to 10 minutes before serving. Use a metal spatula to dislodge the zuppa. Cut into individual portions and serve hot or warm.

VERSIONE CON FINOCCHIO (VARIATION WITH FENNEL): Trim the fronds and stalks from 2 large bulbs fennel and slice the bulbs in half lengthwise. Chop the fronds to equal ⅓ cup and lay them aside. Pour 3 cups Vegetable Broth or water into a saucepan and add 1 teaspoon salt. (Using the broth will result in a tastier dish, but if good, flavorful bread is used, the water used for cooking the fennel can be used for pouring over the bread layers.) Bring to a boil, add the fennel, and cook until tender, about 10 minutes. Drain the fennel halves and slice them horizontally. Distribute half of the sliced fennel and chopped fronds atop each layer of soft cheese. Proceed with the recipe as instructed.

VERSIONE CON POMODORO (VARIATION WITH FRESH AND SUN-DRIED TOMATOES): Seed and slice 1 pound vine-ripened tomatoes. Drain 3 ounces sun-dried tomatoes packed in olive oil and chop as finely as possible. (The chopped pieces must be very small, as sun-dried tomatoes are too intensely flavored to be eaten in big pieces.) Distribute both the fresh and dried tomatoes between the layers of bread and soft cheese. Proceed with the recipe as instructed.

*1-½ teaspoons chopped fresh rosemary,*
*or ¾ teaspoon dried rosemary*
*1-½ teaspoons chopped fresh thyme, or*
*¾ teaspoon dried thyme*
*3 to 3-¼ cups Vegetable Broth (page 58)*

# ZUPPA DI PASTA E LENTICCHIE
# DI ANNA AMENDOLARA

❀

ANNA AMENDOLARA'S PASTA AND LENTIL SOUP

FOR 4 PEOPLE

HERE IS ANOTHER OF MY FRIEND ANNA'S IRRESISTIBLE APULIAN RECIPES. THE FLAVOR OF THE SIMPLE LENTIL AND PASTA SOUP IS EXPANDED BY THE ADDITIONS OF EXTRA-VIRGIN OLIVE OIL AND VEGETABLES. THE LENTILS DO NOT NEED TO BE REHYDRATED BEFORE COOKING.

*6 cups water*

*1-¼ cups ( ½ pound) dried lentils, rinsed and picked over*

*1 large onion, finely chopped*

*1 large carrot, scraped and cut into small dice*

*2 celery stalks, leaves removed, cut into small dice*

*1 large clove garlic, finely chopped*

*1-½ cups canned tomatoes in purée, coarsely chopped*

*¼ cup extra-virgin olive oil*

*1 teaspoon salt, plus salt to taste*

*¼ pound spaghetti, broken into 1-inch lengths*

*¼ teaspoon coarsely ground freshly milled black pepper*

In a soup kettle, combine the water, lentils, onion, carrot, celery, garlic, and tomatoes. Add the olive oil, cover, and bring to a boil over high heat. Reduce the heat to medium-low and simmer, partially covered, until the lentils are tender, about 1 hour.

Meanwhile, fill a saucepan with water and bring to a boil. Add the 1 teaspoon salt and the spaghetti and cook until tender but still quite firm (*al dente*), about 7 minutes. Drain the pasta and add it to the lentils. Season with salt to taste and the pepper.

Ladle the soup into individual bowls. Serve immediately.

AHEAD-OF-TIME NOTE: The soup can be made in advance, but the pasta must not be added until serving time or it will overcook. Prepare the soup up to the point where the pasta is added. Cool, cover, and refrigerate the soup for 2 or 3 days. At serving time, cook the pasta and add it to the reheated soup. The soup also freezes well, as long as the pasta is not added beforehand.

# ZUPPA DI SCAROLA

✸

ESCAROLE SOUP WITH OLIVE OIL CROUTONS

FOR 6 PEOPLE

I HAVE ALWAYS LOVED THIS SOUP, ESPECIALLY THE LOVELY CONTRAST OF THE SIZZLING HOT CROUTONS WITH THE SWEETNESS OF THE COOKED ESCAROLE. MY MOTHER ALWAYS MADE IT ON THANKSGIVING AS A FIRST COURSE TO PRECEDE THE TURKEY. IT IS USUALLY MADE WITH A CHICKEN BROTH IN THE ITALIAN KITCHEN. USING A VEGETABLE BROTH EASILY CONVERTS IT TO A VEGETARIAN SOUP.

Remove and discard any wilted outer leaves of the escarole. Cut off the tough bottom and trim off any brown spots. Wash the escarole well to remove any sand trapped in the leaves. Cut into ribbons ½ inch wide.

In a saucepan bring the broth to a boil. Add the escarole and allow the soup to return to a boil. Reduce the heat to medium-low and simmer, uncovered, until tender, 5 to 7 minutes. Taste for salt.

Meanwhile, in a skillet over medium-high heat, warm the olive oil. When it is hot enough to make a piece of bread sizzle, add the diced bread and fry until golden on both sides. This will have to be done in batches if the skillet is too small to accommodate all the bread cubes without crowding.

While the bread is frying, ladle the soup into individual bowls. Toss the hot croutons into the hot soup (they should sizzle). Pass the pepper and *parmigiano* at the table. The soup should be eaten piping hot.

*1 small head (1-¼ pounds) escarole or curly endive*

*8 cups (2 quarts) Vegetable Broth (page 58)*

*salt*

*2 cups diced Italian or French bread (½-inch dice)*

*1 cup extra-virgin olive oil*

*freshly milled black or white pepper*

*freshly grated parmigiano*

# ZUPPA DI CECI E FINOCCHIO ALLA SARDA

❁

SARDINIAN CHICK-PEA AND FENNEL SOUP

FOR 6 PEOPLE

O N THE REMOTE ISLAND OF SARDINIA, **PASTA E FAGIOLI** TAKES THE FORM OF A CHICK-PEA, WILD FENNEL, AND PASTA SOUP. EITHER THE COUSCOUSLIKE PASTA CALLED **FREGULA** OR A TUBULAR SOUP PASTA IS USED. WILD FENNEL IS NOT AVAILABLE IN AMERICA, BUT CULTIVATED FENNEL CAN BE SUBSTITUTED SUCCESSFULLY. ALSO, BECAUSE SARDINIA IS A LAND OF SHEPHERDS, SLIVERS OF FRESH **PECORINO** ARE SPRINKLED OVER THE BOWLS OF SOUP JUST BEFORE THEY ARE SERVED. (**PARMIGIANO** CAN BE SUBSTITUTED FOR THE **PECORINO**.) CHICK-PEAS ARE OFTEN VERY HARD IN THEIR DRIED FORM, REQUIRING LONGER SOAKING THAN OTHER BEANS. THEY MUST BE SOAKED OVERNIGHT, OR EVEN LONGER, FOR BEST RESULTS. FOR A QUICKER DISH, USE CANNED CHICK-PEAS. OTHER BEANS SUCH AS **CANNELLINI**, NAVY BEANS, OR CRANBERRY BEANS CAN BE SUBSTITUTED. ❁ IN THE NONVEGETARIAN VERSION, A HAM BONE GIVES THIS SOUP A GREAT DEAL OF FLAVOR. ITS ABSENCE, HOWEVER, ALLOWS THE DISTINCTIVE FLAVORS OF THE OTHER INGREDIENTS TO SHINE.

*2-½ cups (two 16-ounce cans) chick-peas, rinsed and drained*

*3 tablespoons extra-virgin olive oil*

*1 onion, chopped*

*1 large clove garlic, chopped*

*2 tablespoons plus 1 teaspoon chopped fresh Italian parsley*

*1 large bulb fennel, stalks and fronds removed, halved, cored, and thinly sliced crosswise (about 2 cups)*

*3 tablespoons minced fresh fennel fronds*

*1 large boiling or baking potato, peeled and cut into small dice*

*2 cups peeled, seeded, and chopped fresh or canned plum tomatoes*

*1 tablespoon salt*

*¼ teaspoon freshly milled black pepper*

Rinse the chick-peas in cold water and drain. In a soup kettle over low heat, warm the oil. Add the onion, garlic, and the 2 tablespoons parsley; cover and cook gently, stirring occasionally, until the vegetables are lightly colored, about 5 minutes. Remove the cover and add the fennel bulb and fronds and potato and sauté for an additional 10 minutes. Add the tomatoes, salt, and pepper, and then the chick-peas and boiling water. Stir well, cover, and cook for 10 minutes over medium heat. Add the pasta and salt and continue to simmer, uncovered, stirring occasionally, until the pasta is just tender, about 10 minutes longer. Taste and correct for salt and pepper. Remove from the heat.

Stir in the 1 teaspoon parsley and the ¼ cup cheese. Ladle the soup into individual bowls and serve. Pass additional cheese at the table.

VARIATION WITH ROSEMARY: To the tomatoes in the skillet, add 1 heaping tablespoon of tomato paste, then the salt and pepper. In a blender or with a potato masher, crush half of the chickpeas. Add them and the remaining whole chickpeas to the skillet with 7 cups of boiling stock or water. Stir in 1 tablespoon chopped fresh rosemary leaves, or 1 teaspoon dried rosemary. Proceed as directed in the recipe.

AHEAD-OF-TIME NOTE: The soup can be made in advance, but the pasta must not be added until serving time or it will overcook. Prepare the soup up to the point where the pasta is added. Cool, cover, and refrigerate the soup for 2 or 3 days. At serving time, cook the pasta and add it, the last 1 teaspoon parsley, and the cheese to the reheated soup. The soup also freezes well, as long as the pasta and cheese are not added beforehand.

6 cups water, boiling

1 tablespoon salt, or to taste

freshly milled black pepper

1 cup ditalini ("little thimbles") pasta

¼ cup coarsely grated or shredded fior di Sardegna or other mild sheep's milk cheese, plus additional cheese for the table

# FARFALLE ALLA LIGURE

❊

FRESH "BUTTERFLIES" WITH PINE NUTS AND MARJORAM

FOR 4 TO 6 PEOPLE

HERE IS A VARIATION ON A TRADITIONAL LIGURIAN DISH OF HOMEMADE FIGURE-EIGHT SHAPED PASTA CALLED **CORZETTI**, **CROSETTI**, OR EVEN **COLZETTI**. **CORZETTI** ARE FORMED BY PINCHING OFF MARBLE-SIZED PIECES OF THE PASTA DOUGH, PULLING IT WITH THE FINGERS INTO LONG, THIN PIECES, AND THEN FLATTENING THEM AT EACH END TO FORM A FIGURE-EIGHT. THE PASTA IS TOSSED WITH A SIMPLE SAUCE OF SWEET BUTTER, TOASTED CHOPPED **PINOLI** (PINE NUTS), AND FRESH MARJORAM. FRESH **FARFALLE**—"BUTTERFLIES"—ARE SOMETIMES USED IN THIS DISH INSTEAD OF **CORZETTI**. THE SAUCE IS ALSO SUITABLE FOR HOMEMADE **TAGLIATELLE**. WHILE IT IS TRADITIONALLY USED ON FRESH PASTA, THE SAUCE WOULD ALSO BE SUITABLE FOR LIGHT DRIED PASTA CUTS SUCH AS **FARFALLE**, SPAGHETTI, AND CERTAIN EGG NOODLES. ❊ THE ONLY KIND OF MACHINE TO USE FOR MAKING AUTHENTIC FRESH PASTA IS A ROLLER-TYPE PASTA MACHINE. EXTRUSION MACHINES AND PASTA ATTACHMENTS ON OTHER KITCHEN EQUIPMENT DO NOT ALLOW FOR PROPER KNEADING AND ROLLING OF THE DOUGH. AFTER BEING PASSED THROUGH THE ROLLERS, THE DOUGH IS CUT BY HAND INTO SMALL SQUARES, THEN PINCHED INTO BUTTERFLY SHAPES.

*For the pasta dough (makes about 1-½ pounds):*

*2 cups unbleached all-purpose flour*

*⅛ teaspoon salt*

*2 jumbo eggs or 4 large eggs*

*1 tablespoon olive oil or oil without flavor, such as safflower or corn oil*

*For cooking the pasta:*

*6 quarts water*

*2 tablespoons salt*

To prepare the pasta, measure the flour and salt directly onto a large pastry board or kitchen work surface. Make a well in the center of the flour. In a small bowl, lightly beat the eggs with the oil. Pour the wet ingredients into the well. Using a fork, beat the egg mixture to combine the ingredients and then gradually draw in the flour from the inside of the well. Always gently beat with the fork in the same direction to prevent air pockets from forming holes in the dough later. Do not let the egg mixture run out of the well. Protect the outside wall with the hand not holding the fork until the wet mixture is well enough integrated with the flour not to stream out. When the mixture is too stiff to use the fork any longer, scrape the dough from the fork into the well and continue forming the dough with your hands.

When you have formed a very soft ball of dough, use a pastry scraper to sweep up the flour left on the board. Sift it, discarding all the dried-out dough bits. The object is to form a uniform, smooth, soft ball of dough. Add only enough of the sifted flour to form a firm yet very pliable dough; the dough should not be hard. The perfect consistency is soft but not sticky, and responsive to being worked with. The amount of flour will depend on how much the eggs absorb and on the humidity in the room, so more or less flour may be required.

Flatten the ball of dough on the board and, using the heels of your hands, knead it from the middle of the disk outward, folding it in half after you work it each time. Do this for about 10 minutes, or until a smooth, elastic dough is formed. Be sure to knead the dough on both sides, working it through and through while keeping it basically round. Well-kneaded dough makes rolling and cutting easy, and produces a noodle that is tender but firm. Work quickly and do not let the dough rest unnecessarily. Cover the dough ball with an inverted bowl or slightly damp kitchen towel to prevent a crust from forming on its surface.

Set up your pasta machine so that everything on your work surface is within easy reach. Divide the dough into 6 equal portions. With your hands or a standard rolling pin, flatten the piece you are working with; keep the others covered. Dust it lightly with flour. Set the machine at the widest possible setting for rolling. Feed the dough through the roller without pulling it or stretching it. Drape it over your hand with your thumb up in the air to avoid sticking your fingers through it. Fold it in thirds as you would a letter, overlapping the top third, and then the bottom third, over the middle third. (This will keep the piece of dough in a uniform rectangular shape, which is important as you roll it out thinner and longer.) Press the dough flat with your hands and fingertips to get all the air out and lightly flour one side only (the other side remains unfloured so that it will adhere to itself when you fold it in thirds again). Set the rollers one notch past the previous one. Pass the dough through again, collecting it at the other end. Repeat the process of folding the strip of dough in thirds and pressing out the air, flouring it lightly on one side, then putting it through the second notch, for a total of 3 times (more, up to 8 times, if you did not knead the dough for at least 10 minutes). Then feed the flattened piece of dough, narrow end first, through the machine's rollers at each remaining setting. Dust the sheet of dough with flour on both sides as necessary to prevent sticking. For *farfalle*, the dough must be as thin as possible, so it must pass through the last setting on the machine. When the whole length of the sheet has passed through the rollers for the last time, collect it carefully with your hands and pull it to its full length, freeing it of folds. Set the strip aside and cover with clean kitchen towels. Roll

For the sauce:

10 tablespoons unsalted butter

½ cup pine nuts, lightly toasted and roughly chopped

½ cup freshly grated parmigiano, *plus* additional parmigiano *for the table*

2 tablespoons chopped fresh marjoram

freshly milled white pepper

out each portion completely in this same manner, covering them well until all the dough is passed through the machine.

To form the *farfalle*, using a fluted pastry wheel, cut each sheet of pasta in half lengthwise. Then cut every 2 inches across the width of each strip to form rectangles about 2 inches long and 1 inch wide. Using your thumb and forefinger, press two opposite long sides together, pinching firmly in the middle so that a bow is formed. Line several baking sheets with clean kitchen towels. Place the *farfalle* on the towels and allow them to dry for 10 minutes. (At this point, they can be covered with dry kitchen towels and set aside for up to several hours before cooking, if desired.)

To cook the pasta, bring the water to a rolling boil in a large pot. Pick up each of the towels holding the *farfalle* by two opposite corners, so the contents can be easily and quickly dumped into the boiling water. Dump all of the *farfalle* into the boiling water as quickly as possible so all the pasta begins cooking at the same time. Stir immediately and add the salt to the water. Stir well again and cover. When the pasta rises to the surface, it is cooked, about 1 minute from the time the water returns to the boil. Be certain not to overcook; the entire cooking process should take no longer than 3 to 4 minutes.

Meanwhile, to make the sauce, melt the butter in a skillet large enough to accommodate the pasta later. Drain the *farfalle*, transfer them to the skillet, and toss with the butter. Using two large forks and keeping the gentlest possible flame under the skillet, distribute the sauce well through the pasta. Add the pine nuts, the ½ cup cheese, the marjoram, and pepper to taste and serve immediately. Pass additional *parmigiano* at the table.

# FETTUCCINE AL PESTO

✸

### FETTUCCINE WITH BASIL SAUCE

FOR 4 OR 5 PEOPLE

**A**LTHOUGH THE TRADITIONAL TYPE OF PASTA MATED WITH **PESTO** IN LIGURIA IS THICK HOME-MADE EGGLESS NOODLES CALLED **TRENETTE**, MY PERSONAL PREFERENCE FOR **PESTO** IS FRESH PASTA MADE WITH EGGS SUCH AS **FETTUCCINE** AND **TONNARELLI** (EGG NOODLES THICKER THAN **FETTUCCINE**). THE RECIPE METHOD GIVES INSTRUCTIONS FOR **FETTUCCINE**, BUT **TONNARELLI**, WHICH ARE IN FACT QUITE LIKE THE TRADITONAL **TRENETTE**, CAN BE MADE BY PASSING THE DOUGH ONLY UP THROUGH THE NEXT-TO-LAST SETTING ON THE MACHINE AND THEN CUTTING IT WITH THE SAME ATTACHMENT USED FOR **FETTUCCINE**. ✸ READERS SHOULD NOTE THAT **PESTO** IS NOT MATED ARBITRARILY WITH ANY SHAPE OF PASTA IN ITALY, AS IT IS IN AMERICA. NOR IS IT MIXED WITH THINGS LIKE CHICKEN OR PIZZA. THE UNCTUOUS NATURE OF **PESTO** REQUIRES A THICK, STURDY CUT TO SUPPORT IT. THIS IS PRECISELY THE REASON FOR THE TRADITIONAL MATCH WITH **TRENETTE**. ✸ SPAGHETTI IS THE LIGHTEST CUT THAT SHOULD BE SERVED WITH **PESTO**, BUT THE BEST DRIED CUT FOR THIS SAUCE IS **LINGUINE**. **PESTO** SHOULD NEVER BE SERVED WITH FINE CUTS SUCH AS ANGEL'S HAIR, BECAUSE SUCH VARIETIES SIMPLY DON'T ALLOW THE SAUCE TO BECOME DISTRIBUTED THROUGH THEIR DELICATE STRANDS; THE SAUCE JUST COLLECTS UNDER RATHER THAN THROUGHOUT THE MASS OF PASTA. ✸ THE CLASSIC **PESTO** OF GENOA CONTAINS ONLY BASIL, **PINOLI** (PINE NUTS), OLIVE OIL, BUTTER, GARLIC, AND GRATED CHEESE (**PARMIGIANO** OR **PECORINO,** OR A COMBINATION OF THE TWO). MY MOTHER OFTEN COMBINES BASIL WITH PARSLEY WHEN SHE MAKES **PESTO** (ADMITTEDLY, SHE IS NOT FROM GENOA, ALTHOUGH SHE LIVED THERE BRIEFLY BEFORE MARRYING AND WAS INSPIRED TO ADD A GENOESE DISH OR TWO TO HER CULINARY REPERTOIRE). WHILE THIS IS A DEPARTURE FROM THE AUTHENTIC METHOD, I LIKE IT BECAUSE THE ADDITION OF PARSLEY CUTS THE SWEETNESS OF THE BASIL, A TASTE THAT I PREFER. IT IS ALSO POSSIBLE TO MAKE **PESTO** WITHOUT THE PINE NUTS, WHICH PRODUCES A LESS UNCTUOUS, BUT LIGHTER SAUCE. WHICHEVER METHOD YOU CHOOSE, IT IS IMPORTANT TO REMEMBER THAT **PESTO** SHOULD NEVER BE COOKED. IT IS ADDED TO PASTA AFTER IT IS COOKED AND DRAINED; THE PASTA IS NEVER RETURNED TO THE HEAT. LIKEWISE, WHEN ADDING A DOLLOP OF **PESTO** TO **MINESTRONE**, IT IS STIRRED IN ONLY WHEN THE SOUP IS FINISHED COOKING, AT THE MOMENT OF SERVING.

*For the* pesto:

3 cloves garlic, cut into pieces

2 cups solidly packed fresh basil leaves,
   or 1 cup each solidly packed fresh
   basil leaves and Italian parsley leaves

¾ teaspoon salt

freshly milled white or black pepper

½ cup extra-virgin olive oil

⅓ cup pine nuts, very lightly toasted

¾ cup freshly grated parmigiano

2 tablespoons unsalted butter, softened to
   room temperature


*For the* pasta:

1 recipe pasta dough (page 70)


*For cooking the* pasta:

6 quarts water

2 tablespoons salt


1 tablespoon unsalted butter, softened to
   room temperature for serving

To make the *pesto*, put the garlic pieces, basil leaves, salt, pepper to taste, oil, and pine nuts into a food processor fitted with the metal blade, or into a blender jar. Blend to a smooth purée. Do not overdo the grinding, or your *pesto* will have very little texture. Transfer the mixture to a bowl. Add the *parmigiano* to the bowl and, using a wooden spoon, beat in the cheese by hand until it is fully incorporated. Then beat in the butter, using strong, swift strokes. Cover and set aside.

For the pasta, make the dough according to the instructions on page 70. When the whole length of each sheet has passed through the rollers for the last time, collect it carefully with your hands and pull it to its full length, freeing it of folds. Set the strips aside, covered with clean dry kitchen towels, until all the dough is passed through the machine.

To form the *fettuccine*, pass each sheet of pasta through the *fettuccine* cutting attachment of the pasta machine. Line several baking sheets with clean kitchen towels. Place the *fettuccine* on the towels and allow them to dry for 10 minutes. (At this point, they can be set aside, covered with dry kitchen towels, for up to several hours before cooking, if desired.)

To cook the pasta, bring the water to a rolling boil in a large pot. Pick up each of the towels holding the *fettuccine* by two opposite corners, so the contents can be easily and quickly dumped into the boiling water. Dump all of the *fettuccine* into the boiling water as quickly as possible so all the noodles begin cooking at the same time. Stir immediately and add the salt to the water. Stir well again and cover. When the pasta rises to the surface, it is cooked, about 1 minute from the time the water returns to the boil. Be certain not to overcook; the entire pasta cooking process should take no longer than 3 to 4 minutes.

While the pasta is cooking, spoon 2 tablespoons of the cooking water into a warmed serving bowl large enough to accommodate the pasta later. Add the pesto and the remaining 1 tablespoon butter and beat well with a wooden spoon to blend.

Drain the *fettuccine* and transfer them to the serving bowl holding the *pesto*. Using two large forks, distribute the *pesto* well through the pasta. Serve immediately. KEEPING AND FREEZING PESTO: *Pesto* will keep in the refrigerator or freezer for several months in a sealed glass jar but leave out the cheese, salt, and butter. Push a layer of plastic wrap onto the very surface of the *pesto* to prevent a dark layer from forming on the top. Beat cheese, salt, and butter in just before using the *pesto*.

# SPAGHETTINI AL LIMONE CON LE OLIVE

❋

THIN SPAGHETTI WITH UNCOOKED LEMON AND BLACK OLIVE SAUCE

FOR 4 TO 6 PEOPLE

I LIKE THE SAUCE BECAUSE IT IS ONE OF THE ONLY NONTOMATO SAUCES THAT IS SUITABLE FOR VERY THIN PASTA CUTS SUCH AS **SPAGHETTINI** OR **CAPELLINI**. ❋ THE SAUCE IS UNCOOKED AND TAKES JUST MINUTES TO MAKE. A WORD OF CAUTION, HOWEVER: USE ONLY HIGH QUALITY EXTRA-VIRGIN OLIVE OIL. A BLAND OLIVE OIL WILL NOT GIVE THE SAUCE SUFFICIENT FLAVOR; IT WILL ONLY MAKE THE SPAGHETTI SEEM OILY.

To remove the zest from the lemon, grate the lemon on the small holes of a standard box grater, being sure not to include the bitter white layer just below the oily yellow citrus skin. Use a pastry brush to dislodge the zest that clings to the holes of the grater. Alternatively, use a citrus zester, which can be found in most kitchen specialty shops.

In a warmed serving bowl large enough to accommodate the pasta later, combine the lemon zest, lemon juice, olive oil, garlic cloves, olives, thyme, the 1 teaspoon of salt, and pepper to taste. Press on the garlic with the back of a wooden spoon to release its juices, and remove it just before you add the cooked pasta to the sauce.

To cook the pasta, bring the water to a rolling boil in a large pot. Add the pasta and the 2 tablespoons salt to it. Stir frequently to prevent the pasta from sticking together and continue to cook over high heat. *Capellini* will cook in approximately 3 minutes and *spaghettini* in about 5 minutes. Taste the pasta to determine its doneness; it should be *al dente*, that is, tender but quite firm to the bite. Do not overcook the pasta. If in doubt as to its doneness, drain it immediately, as the pasta continues to cook while it is hot. Take care not to overdrain; the pasta should be piping hot and still dripping when it is transferred to the serving bowl. Reserve some of the pasta cooking water.

Toss the hot pasta with the cold sauce. *Capellini* have a tendency, because of their fineness, to absorb moisture rapidly, and so it is often necessary to return some of the pasta cooking water to the sauce to prevent the *capellini* from clumping; the additional water will help to distribute the sauce easily through the strands. Serve piping hot.

*zest of 1 lemon*

*⅓ cup freshly squeezed lemon juice*

*½ cup plus 2 tablespoons extra-virgin olive oil*

*3 large cloves garlic*

*½ cup sharply flavored black olives, such as Gaeta, Niçoise or Kalamata olives, pitted and sliced*

*2 tablespoons chopped fresh thyme, or 1-½ teaspoons dried thyme*

*1 teaspoon plus 2 tablespoons salt*

*plenty of freshly milled white or black pepper*

*6 quarts water*

*1 pound* spaghettini *(thin spaghetti)* or capellini

# PENNETTE CON MELANZANE ALLA GIUSTINA

✦

GIUSTINA'S LITTLE PENNE WITH EGGPLANT

FOR 2 OR 3 PEOPLE

THERE ARE MANY WAYS OF COOKING EGGPLANT FOR PASTA. THIS RECIPE, MY MOTHER'S CREATION, IS UNUSUAL BECAUSE IT CONTAINS WINE VINEGAR, WHICH GIVES A NICE LITTLE TANG TO THE SAUCE. A MEDIUM-SIZED PASTA CUT THAT IS STURDY ENOUGH TO SUPPORT THE SAUCE SHOULD BE USED; **PENNETTE** ("LITTLE QUILLS") ARE A GOOD CHOICE. SHAPES SUCH AS **CRESTE DI GALLO** ("COCKSCOMBS"), **GEMELLI** ("TWINS"), **CONCHIGLIE** ("SHELLS"), AND **GNOCCHETTI** ("LITTLE DUMPLINGS") ARE ALSO SUITABLE, AND WILL CRADLE THE SAUCE IN THEIR GROOVES OR HOLLOWS.

Peel the eggplant and cut it into 1-inch dice. Place the cubes in a colander and sprinkle with salt. Place the colander in the sink or over a dish and let it stand so the bitter liquid drains out of the seeds, 30 to 40 minutes. Rinse the eggplant in cold water and pat dry with a clean kitchen towel.

Place the oil, onion, and garlic in a cold skillet (preferably nonstick) over medium-low heat. Sauté gently until the onion and garlic are softened but not colored, about 5 minutes. Add the eggplant and marjoram and sauté over medium heat until colored, about 5 minutes. Cover, reduce the heat to low, and cook until the eggplant is tender, 10 to 15 minutes. Stir occasionally to prevent the eggplant from sticking, always replacing the cover.

Meanwhile, bring the water to a rolling boil in a large pot. Add the pasta and 1 tablespoon salt. Stir immediately and continue to cook over high heat, stirring every few minutes to prevent the pasta from sticking together.

When the eggplant is cooked, remove the cover and stir in the parsley, vinegar, and salt and pepper to taste. When the pasta is *al dente* (tender but quite firm to the bite), drain it and, while it is still dripping, transfer it to a warmed serving bowl.

Immediately add the eggplant sauce to the pasta and toss well. Serve at once.

*1 large eggplant (about 1-¾ pounds)*
*salt*
*2 tablespoons extra-virgin olive oil*
*1 small onion, chopped*
*1 large clove garlic, chopped*
*1 teaspoon chopped fresh marjoram, or*
   *½ teaspoon dried marjoram*
*6 quarts water*
*½ pound* penne *("little quills") or*
   *other medium-sized pasta (see*
   *recipe introduction)*
*1 tablespoon chopped fresh Italian parsley*
*1 tablespoon red wine vinegar*
*freshly milled black pepper*

# PASTA E FAGIOLI

✸

PASTA AND BEANS

FOR 4 PEOPLE

**T**HE ORIGINS OF THIS DISH ARE IN THE THICK, RUSTIC MACARONI AND BEAN SOUP MADE WITH DRIED BEANS AND A HAM BONE OR SALT PORK. CHICK-PEAS ARE SOMETIMES USED INSTEAD OF WHITE BEANS. THIS IS A DELICIOUS VEGETARIAN VARIATION AND CAN BE QUICK TO MAKE AS WELL IF THE BEANS ARE ALREADY COOKED. WHEN I WAS GROWING UP, MY FATHER OFTEN STOPPED HOME FOR LUNCH UNEXPECTEDLY; THIS WAS INEVITABLY WHAT MY MOTHER COOKED UP FOR HIM—IN THE LENGTH OF TIME IT TOOK FOR THE PASTA TO BOIL. CANNED BEANS CAN BE SUBSTITUTED FOR COOKED, REHYDRATED DRIED BEANS AS LONG AS THEY CONTAIN NO SUGAR OR OTHER ADDITIVES. THERE IS, HOWEVER, NO SUBSTITUTE FOR FLAVORFUL EXTRA-VIRGIN OLIVE OIL, BECAUSE IN THIS DISH OF ONLY FOUR MAIN INGREDIENTS, THE OIL AND THE ONION ARE THE PRIMARY SOURCES OF FLAVOR. THE DISH CAN BE SERVED AS A FIRST OR MAIN COURSE.

1-⅓ cups (½ pound) dried cannellini or Great Northern beans, or 2 cans (16 ounces each) white beans

5 quarts water

½ pound ditalini ("little thimbles")

1-½ tablespoons salt, plus salt to taste

½ cup extra-virgin olive oil

2 teaspoons chopped fresh rosemary, or 1 teaspoon dried rosemary

1 very large or 2 medium-sized onions, sliced paper-thin

freshly milled black pepper

If using dried beans, rinse them and pick them over and then rehydrate and cook them according to the directions on page 15; drain and set aside. If using canned beans, drain them and then rinse and drain well again; set aside.

In a soup kettle, bring the water to a boil. Add the pasta and the 1-½ tablespoons salt. Stir and continue to cook over high heat until the water returns to a boil, stirring frequently. When the pasta is half-cooked (about 6 minutes), add the drained beans to the pasta pot.

While the pasta and beans are cooking together, in a skillet over medium heat, warm the oil. Add the rosemary and onion and sauté until lightly browned, about 10 minutes. When the pasta is *al dente* (tender but quite firm to the bite), drain it, and, while it is still dripping, transfer to a warmed serving bowl. Add the browned onion and toss well.

Sprinkle liberally with pepper to taste, and add more salt, if desired. Serve at once.

# SPAGHETTI CON SALSA DI POMODORO E OLIVE NERE

✳

SPAGHETTI WITH TOMATO SAUCE AND BLACK OLIVES

FOR 4 TO 6 PEOPLE

THIS SIMPLE, TASTY SAUCE IS MY MOTHER'S RECIPE. SHE USES IT FOR DRIED PASTA DISHES (USUALLY SPAGHETTI, OR MACARONI SHAPES SUCH AS **PENNE** AND **FUSILLI**), FOR PIZZA, AND, IN NON-VEGETARIAN MEALS, AS A CONDIMENT FOR FISH, CHICKEN, OR BOILED BEEF. A SMALL QUANTITY OF FULL-FLAVORED IMPORTED OLIVES ADDS A GREAT DEAL OF FLAVOR TO VEGETARIAN SAUCES; THE BLAND, CANNED VARIETIES ARE SIMPLY NOT SUITABLE. THERE IS NO NEED FOR MORE THAN THE TWO TABLESPOONS CALLED FOR IN THIS RECIPE, AS A LARGER QUANTITY WOULD OVERPOWER THE SAUCE. IF YOU WISH TO USE THE SAUCE FOR PIZZA, HOWEVER, THE OLIVES CAN BE DOUBLED.

In a saucepan over medium-low heat, warm the oil. Add the garlic and onion and sauté gently until the vegetables are wilted, about 5 minutes. Stir in the tomato paste and allow it to heat gently for 2 to 3 minutes. Add the olives and parsley. Stir well, then stir in the tomatoes, the ½ teaspoon salt, and the ¾ cup water. Partially cover and allow the sauce to simmer gently for 20 minutes, stirring occasionally

Meanwhile, bring 6 quarts water to a rolling boil in a large pot. Add the spaghetti and the 2 tablespoons salt. Stir immediately and continue to cook over high heat until the water returns to a boil. Keep the heat on high and stir frequently to prevent the pasta from sticking together. When the spaghetti is *al dente* (tender but quite firm to the bite), drain it immediately. Transfer it to a warmed serving bowl.

Immediately add the sauce to the pasta and toss well. Serve at once.

*2 tablespoons extra-virgin olive oil*

*1 large clove garlic, finely chopped*

*2 tablespoons finely chopped onion*

*3 level tablespoons tomato paste*

*2 tablespoons sliced, pitted imported black olives, such as Gaeta, Niçoise, or Kalamata*

*2 tablespoons chopped fresh Italian parsley*

*½ teaspoon plus 2 tablespoons salt*

*¾ cup plus 6 quarts water*

*1 can (28 ounces) crushed tomatoes, or 2-½ cups peeled, seeded, and chopped vine-ripened tomatoes (2-½ pounds)*

*1 pound spaghetti*

*2 tablespoons salt*

# SPAGHETTI CON SALSA DI NOCI ALLA SARDA

❋

SPAGHETTI WITH WALNUT SAUCE, SARDINIA STYLE

FOR 4 TO 6 PEOPLE

ACCORDING TO SARDINIAN WRITER FERNANDO PILIA, THIS DISH PREDATES THE APPEARANCE OF TOMATOES IN ITALY. TOMATOES WERE CONSIDERED POISONOUS BY THE EUROPEANS UNTIL THE MID-EIGHTEENTH CENTURY. THE SAUCE CAN BE MADE IN THE TIME IT TAKES FOR THE PASTA TO COOK. THE GROUND NUTS PRODUCE A VERY CREAMY, UNCTUOUS SAUCE NOT UNLIKE **PESTO** IN TEXTURE THAT NEEDS A STURDY CUT TO SUPPORT IT. THIS IS A SAUCE DESIGNED FOR THE TEXTURE OF **PASTA SECCA** ("DRIED PASTA"), NOT DELICATE HOMEMADE EGG PASTA. NO CUT THINNER THAN SPAGHETTI SHOULD BE USED FOR THIS DISH; **FETTUCCINE, LINGUINE,** OR **BUCATINI** WOULD CARRY THE SAUCE OFF WELL.

*½ cup walnuts*

*⅓ cup extra-virgin olive oil*

*2 large cloves garlic, finely chopped*

*1 tablespoon chopped fresh Italian parsley*

*6 quarts water*

*2 tablespoons salt*

*1 pound spaghetti or other pasta*
  *(see recipe introduction)*

*1 cup reserved pasta cooking water*

*1 cup (¼ pound) freshly grated* fior di
  Sardegna *or* Tuscan caciotta

Grind the walnuts in a food processor until they are fairly finely ground but not pasty. Be careful not to grind too long or the oil in the nuts will be released. In a skillet large enough to accommodate the cooked pasta later, heat together the ground nuts, olive oil, garlic, and parsley over gentle heat until the garlic is softened but not colored, about 7 minutes. Remove the skillet from the heat and set aside.

Meanwhile, bring the water to a rolling boil in a large pot. Add the pasta and salt. Stir immediately and continue to cook over high heat until the water returns to a boil. Keep the heat on high and stir frequently to prevent the pasta from sticking together. When the pasta is not quite *al dente* (still slightly undercooked), drain it, reserving 1 cup of the cooking water. While the pasta is still dripping, transfer it to the skillet with the sauce. Using two large forks and keeping the gentlest possible heat under the skillet, distribute the sauce well through pasta. Add as much of the 1 cup reserved cooking water as you need to moisten the sauce, adding it little by little; it is not likely that you will need more than ½ cup of it.

Add the cheese to the pasta, toss, then remove from the heat and transfer to a warmed serving bowl. Serve immediately.

# ABOUT RISOTTO

A GOOD **RISOTTO** IS A SIMPLE DISH TO MAKE IF THESE THINGS ARE REMEMBERED: USE AUTHENTIC ITALIAN ARBORIO, VIALONE NANO, OR CARNAROLI RICE (LONG-GRAIN RICE CAN BE SUBSTITUTED, BUT IT WON'T PRODUCE A **RISOTTO** AS TASTY OR CREAMY); AS ALWAYS IN ITALIAN COOKING, EMPLOY THE BEST AND PUREST INGREDIENTS POSSIBLE; BE SURE THE BROTH IS HOT (COLD LIQUID WILL BRING DOWN THE TEMPERATURE), AND THAT IT IS ADDED ONLY ONE LADLEFUL AT A TIME AND THEN FULLY ABSORBED BEFORE THE NEXT LADLEFUL IS ADDED; AND LASTLY, STIR THE RICE CONSTANTLY AS IT IS COOKING. **RISOTTO** IS UNLIKE OTHER RICE DISHES IN THAT THE CONSISTENCY IS ALWAYS CREAMY (ALTHOUGH NOT RUNNY), AND NEVER DRY OR STICKY. THIS CREAMINESS IS A RESULT OF THE UNUSUAL PROPERTIES OF ARBORIO AND SIMILAR ITALIAN RICE VARIETIES, AND ALSO A PRODUCT OF THE COOKING METHOD: HOT BROTH IS ADDED LITTLE BY LITTLE, ALLOWING THE GRAINS TO INCORPORATE THE MOISTURE AND FLAVORS OF THE OTHER INGREDIENTS AND BIND THEM TOGETHER; AT THE SAME TIME, A SEPARATE, PLEASANTLY FIRM TEXTURE IS RETAINED.

# RISOTTO ALLA MILANESE VEGETALE

VEGETARIAN RISOTTO, MILAN STYLE

FOR 6 PEOPLE

THE CLASSIC **RISOTTO ALLA MILANESE** IS BASED ON BUTTER, BEEF MARROW, AND BEEF BROTH, WHICH COMBINED GIVE THE RICE ENORMOUS FLAVOR. I HAVE DEVISED A SIMILAR **RISOTTO** USING MY VEGETABLE BROTH. BEING VERY RICH IN VEGETABLE FLAVORS, THE BROTH IS QUITE SWEET. IT MARRIES WELL WITH THE BUTTER AND SAFFRON HERE AND, DESPITE THE DEPARTURE FROM THE TRADITIONAL INGREDIENTS, THE DISH IS VERY SUCCESSFUL.

*6 cups Vegetable Broth (page 58)*
*6 tablespoons unsalted butter*
*1 onion, chopped*
*2 cups Arborio or similar imported Italian rice*
*½ cup dry white wine*

Place the broth in a saucepan and bring it to a simmer. Reduce the heat to low to keep the broth hot.

Meanwhile, in a deep skillet over medium heat, melt 3 tablespoons of the butter. Add the onion and sauté until softened but not colored, about 5 minutes. Add the rice and increase the heat to high; sauté for 1 to 2 minutes, stirring to coat the grains well. Stir in the wine and reduce the heat to medium. Allow the wine to evaporate and become absorbed, about 3 minutes.

Now add a ladleful of the hot broth, stirring well. When it is nearly all absorbed into the rice, add another ladleful of the hot broth, stirring all the while. Continue in this fashion until the broth is absorbed and the rice is about half-cooked (about 15 minutes), stirring continuously. While the rice is cooking to this point, in a small cup dissolve the saffron in a ladleful of the hot broth. Now add the saffron mixture to the rice and continue cooking as described, stirring continuously, adding only a ladleful of hot broth at a time and waiting until it is absorbed before adding the next ladleful. When the rice is tender but still slightly chewy—it should be creamy, but not mushy—remove from the heat (you may not need to use all the broth). The total cooking time of the rice is from 20 to 25 minutes.

Stir in the remaining 3 tablespoons butter and the ½ cup cheese. Taste for salt and pepper. Serve the finished *risotto* piping hot directly from the hot skillet onto individual plates. Pass additional *parmigiano* at the table.

VERSIONE CON VERDURE (VARIATION WITH VEGETABLES): Either salted water or broth can be used here. Of course broth will produce a tastier *risotto*, but garlic, celery, sweet pepper, and tomatoes enrich the flavor of the *risotto* sufficiently to allow for a tasty *risotto* even if it is made with water. Heat the broth or salted water as directed. To the onion in the skillet add 1 large clove garlic, finely chopped; ½ cup finely chopped celery heart, including 1 tablespoon chopped young celery leaves; and 1 small red or yellow bell pepper, seeded and chopped. Sauté over medium-low heat, stirring occasionally, until all the vegetables are softened but not browned, about 10 minutes. Add the rice and sauté it with the vegetables over medium heat for about 2 minutes, stirring frequently. In place of the wine, stir in 1 cup peeled, seeded, and coarsley chopped fresh or canned tomatoes, plus ½ cup of their juices. Proceed with the recipe until it is time to add the cheese. (Dissolve the saffron in a ladleful of the hot water the same way you would if you were using broth.) Stir in 1-½ tablespoons chopped fresh basil or Italian parsley, only ¼ cup grated *parmigiano*, and ½ cup finely diced mozzarella just before serving. Pass additional grated cheese at the table if you like.

*generous ½ teaspoon saffron filaments,
   or 2 packets (⅛ teaspoon each) pure
   saffron powder*
*salt*
*freshly milled white pepper*
*½ cup freshly grated parmigiano, plus
   additional parmigiano for the
   table*

# RISOTTO AI FUNGHI

❀

WILD MUSHROOM RISOTTO

FOR 6 PEOPLE

I F NOT USING FRESH **PORCINI**, A RARE FIND IN AMERICA, IT IS BEST TO MIX VARIETIES OF WILD MUSH-
ROOMS FOR THIS DISH. TRY THIS DISH WITH THE VARIETIES OF WILD MUSHROOMS AVAILABLE TO
YOU (SEE PAGES 19 AND 21 FOR EXTENSIVE INFORMATION ABOUT WILD MUSHROOM VARIETIES). IF YOU
HAVE ANY LEFTOVER **RISOTTO**, IT MAKES MARVELOUS **CROQUETTES** (PAGE 86).

*5-½ cups Vegetable Broth (page 58)*

*1 pound fresh wild mushrooms (see
recipe introduction)*

*6 tablespoons unsalted butter*

*1 onion, chopped*

*1 large clove garlic, finely chopped*

*2 cups Arborio or similar imported
Italian rice*

*½ cup dry white or red wine*

*2 tablespoons chopped fresh Italian
parsley*

*½ cup freshly grated parmigiano, plus
additional parmigiano for the
table*

*salt*

*freshly milled white or black pepper*

Place the broth in a saucepan and bring to a simmer. Reduce the heat to low.

Meanwhile, remove any dirt from the mushrooms with a soft brush or clean, dry kitchen towel. Trim off the tough bottoms from the stems. If the mushrooms are extremely large, halve or quarter them lengthwise. Set aside.

In a skillet over medium heat, melt 4 tablespoons of the butter. Add the mushrooms and sauté until tender, about 10 minutes. The cooking time will depend upon the variety of mushrooms. Remove from the heat and set aside.

In a large skillet over medium heat, melt the remaining 2 tablespoons butter. Add the onion and garlic and sauté until softened but not colored, about 5 minutes. Add the rice and sauté over medium-high heat for 1 to 2 minutes, stirring to coat the grains well. Stir in the wine, reduce the heat to medium, and allow it to evaporate and become absorbed, about 3 minutes.

Now add a ladleful of the hot broth, stirring well. When it is nearly all absorbed into the rice, add another ladle of the hot broth, stirring all the while. Continue in this fashion until the broth is absorbed and the rice is half-cooked (about 15 minutes), stirring continuously. At this point, stir in half the mushrooms. Continue cooking the rice as described, adding a ladleful of hot broth at a time, stirring all the while and waiting until it is absorbed before adding the next ladleful. When the rice is tender but still slightly chewy—it should be creamy, but not mushy—remove from the heat (you may not need to use all the broth). The total cooking time of the rice is from 20 to 25 minutes.

Stir in the remaining mushrooms, the parsley, and the ½ cup cheese. Taste for salt and pepper. Serve the finished *risotto* piping hot directly from the hot skillet onto individual plates. Pass additional *parmigiano* at the table.

# CROCCHETTE DI RISO COI FUNGHI

❁

RICE CROQUETTES

FOR 8 TO 10 PEOPLE

**M**Y BOOK **ANTIPASTI: THE LITTLE DISHES OF ITALY** GOES INTO DETAIL ABOUT THESE POPULAR ITAL-
IAN RICE BALLS THAT TRAVEL UNDER VARIOUS NAMES: **SUPPLÌ AL TELEFONO** IN ROME, **ARANCINI** IN
SICILY, AND, IN GENERAL, **CROCCHETTE DI RISO**. I MADE UP THIS RECIPE ONE DAY WHEN I HAD SOME LEFT-
OVER MUSHROOM **RISOTTO**. THE CROQUETTES ARE TASTY EVEN WITHOUT THE ADDITION OF TOMATO SAUCE
IN THE MIXTURE, AN INGREDIENT IN MANY SUCH RICE RECIPES. IF DESIRED, THEY CAN BE SERVED WITH A
LIGHT TOMATO SAUCE ON THE SIDE (PAGES 101–102), BUT THEY ARE DELECTABLE AS THEY ARE.

*1 recipe Wild Mushroom Risotto
(page 84)*

*1 extra-large or jumbo egg, plus 2
extra-large or jumbo egg yolks*

*½ pound mozzarella, cut into ½-inch
cubes*

*olive oil for deep-frying*

*2 egg whites*

*about 1 cup fine dried bread crumbs,
lightly toasted (page 17)*

Prepare the *risotto* and then allow it to cool to room temperature.

In a small bowl, beat the whole egg and egg yolks well with a fork, then stir
them into the cooled *risotto*. Cover and chill for at least 2 hours or overnight.

Form spoonfuls of the chilled *risotto* into log shapes about 2 inches long and 1
inch thick, stuffing the center of each with a few pieces of the diced mozzarella
(the croquettes should not be too large). You should have about 15 croquettes
in all.

In a deep skillet, pour in olive oil to a depth of about 2 inches. Heat the oil to
350 degrees F, or until a crust of bread turns golden within seconds of being
dropped into it. Preheat an oven to 250 degrees F. Place the egg whites in a shallow bowl and beat lightly with a fork. Place the bread crumbs in a shallow dish.

Just before frying each croquette, dip it into the egg whites, then roll it in the
bread crumbs. (The croquettes should not be rolled in the crumbs until the last
minute, or they will not be properly crisp when fried.) Carefully slip the croquettes into the hot oil. Do not crowd the pan or the temperature of the oil will
drop. Fry until golden on all sides, turning as necessary, just a few minutes.
Remove with a slotted utensil to paper towels to drain, then keep the croquettes
warm in the oven while you fry the remaining croquettes.

Arrange the croquettes on a warmed platter. Serve piping hot.

AHEAD-OF-TIME NOTE: The croquettes can be fried in advance, covered,
cooled, and refrigerated for 1 to 2 days. Reheat, uncovered, in an oven preheated
to 350 degrees F for 15 to 20 minutes.

# RISOTTO AGLI SPINACI

❊

SPINACH RISOTTO

FOR 6 PEOPLE

**T**HE SPINACH IS ADDED TO THIS **RISOTTO** NEAR THE END OF COOKING SO THAT IT REMAINS BRIGHT GREEN AND RETAINS ITS TEXTURE.  SWISS CHARD CAN ALSO BE USED.

Wash the spinach thoroughly in several changes of water to remove any sand. Discard any yellow leaves; cut off and discard the stems.  Drain but do not dry the spinach leaves.

Cook the spinach in either of two ways:  In a large skillet over medium-low heat, melt the 1 tablespoon butter.  Add the spinach, cover, and steam, turning and tossing it occasionally to cook it evenly, until it is just tender, about 5 minutes. Alternatively, place on a steamer rack, cover, and cook over gently boiling water until wilted but not overly cooked, about 5 minutes.  Remove the spinach to a cutting board and, when cool enough to handle, chop it finely.  Set it aside.  (The spinach will be very moist, but it is not necessary to squeeze out excess liquid.)

Meanwhile, place the broth in a saucepan and bring to a simmer.  Reduce the heat to low to keep the broth hot.

In a large skillet over medium heat, melt 3 tablespoons of the butter.  Add the onion and sauté until softened but not colored, about 5 minutes.  Turn the heat up to medium-high and add the rice and continue to sauté for 1 to 2 minutes, stirring to coat well.  Stir in the wine, reduce the heat to medium, and allow it to evaporate and become absorbed, about 3 minutes.

Now add a ladleful of the hot broth, stirring well.  When it is nearly all absorbed into the rice, add another ladleful of the hot broth, stirring all the while.  Continue in this fashion, stirring frequently, until the rice is nearly cooked (the total cooking time of the rice is from 20 to 25 minutes).  Mix in the spinach.  After about 5 minutes, the rice will be tender but still slightly chewy— it should be creamy, but not mushy.  Remove it from the heat.

Stir in the remaining 3 tablespoons butter and the ½ cup cheese.  Taste for salt and pepper.  Serve the finished *risotto* piping hot directly from the hot skillet onto individual plates.  Pass additional grated *parmigiano* at the table.

*1 pound spinach*

*1 tablespoon unsalted butter, for cooking spinach (optional), plus 6 tablespoons unsalted butter*

*1 onion, chopped*

*2 cups Arborio or similar imported Italian rice*

*½ cup dry white wine*

*6 cups Vegetable Broth (page 58)*

*freshly milled white pepper*

*½ cup freshly grated parmigiano, plus additional parmigiano for the table*

# RISO CON LIMONE ALLA PIEMONTESE

✺

RICE WITH LEMON, PIEDMONT STYLE

FOR 4 TO 6 PEOPLE

THIS IS A SIGNATURE DISH OF PIEDMONT, AND QUITE DIFFERENT FROM A **RISOTTO**. THE RICE IS FIRST BOILED, THEN A RAW EGG AND LEMON SAUCE ARE ADDED WHILE IT IS STILL BOILING HOT. THE HEAT OF THE RICE COOKS THE EGG AND A VELVETY SAUCE RESULTS. THIS RICE CAN BE SERVED AS A FIRST COURSE OR AS A SIDE DISH.

*5 cups water*

*1-½ cups Arborio or similar imported Italian rice*

*1 tablespoon salt*

*3 eggs*

*2 tablespoons freshly squeezed lemon juice*

*1 cup freshly grated parmigiano, plus additional parmigiano for the table*

*freshly milled white pepper*

*3 tablespoons unsalted butter*

In a large saucepan, bring the water to a boil. Meanwhile, in a bowl or pitcher with a pouring spout, combine the rice and salt. Over high heat, add the rice and salt *a pioggia*, that is, "like rain," in a slow, steady stream to prevent the boil from breaking. Reduce the heat to medium and simmer, uncovered, until the rice is cooked, 12 to 15 minutes. Do not stir it as it simmers. The rice should be tender but firm when cooked.

While the rice is cooking, in a bowl beat the eggs until light. Then beat in the lemon juice, the 1 cup cheese, and pepper to taste.

When the rice is cooked, drain it and immediately return it to the saucepan. Add the egg mixture and, using a large spoon, gently mix it thoroughly. Add the butter. Place the pan on a burner over the lowest possible heat for 2 to 3 minutes only, stirring gently several times to distribute the butter throughout.

Serve immediately in a warmed serving bowl with additional *parmigiano* at the table.

chapter four

SECONDI

main courses

THE SECOND COURSE, OR **SECONDO**, IS THE TRADITIONAL MEAT, FOWL, OR FISH COURSE ON THE ITALIAN TABLE. On the vegetarian menu, baked pasta dishes, vegetable or bean casseroles, pies, open-faced tarts, and egg or *polenta* dishes are substantial and interesting enough to satisfy even a profound hunger.

This chapter addresses "big" nonmeat dishes, many of which combine vegetables, protein foods such as eggs, and a carbohydrate in some form. The addition of cheese and eggs to a vegetable dish gives it all the nutritional value of a meat course. Many of the dishes in this chapter fit this category.

Because many second-course vegetarian dishes are starch-based (*polenta*, pasta, and beans, for example), one must be careful to create variety when planning an organized meal. For example, baked pasta, beans, or *polenta* should never be preceded by another type of pasta or a *risotto*. Even soup is never served before a pasta dish, since soup and pasta are both in the first course category. Instead, when serving these *secondi* consider one or more compatible vegetable *antipasti* and skip the *primo* altogether.

Another consideration when planning a vegetarian menu is to create different textures as well as varieties of foods in the various courses. For example, if Eggplant Parmigiana (page 101) is to be the main dish, consider serving a compatible pasta dish as a first course and a crisp green salad as a *contorno*. If serving an egg dish such as Poached Eggs in Tomato Sauce (page 93) or Red Pepper and Onion *Frittata* (page 98), start with a crispy or crunchy *antipasto* such as Lombardian Crispy Deep-Fried *Polenta* Toasts on page 47.

Last, but certainly not least important, when planning a whole menu, combine dishes to get complete nutritional value as well as appealing variety and complementary textures. During the course of the meal, try to serve raw vegetables often in the form of an *antipasto* or a salad. Since eggs are extremely high in protein, avoid beans, which are also loaded with protein, on the same menu. Instead, accompany such high-protein foods with vegetables dishes that are rich in vitamins and contain a great deal of fiber.

Many vegetarian *antipasti* (chapter 2) in increased quantities make suitable main courses. Stuffed vegetables are one of these, as are batter-fried or oven-roasted vegetables. Certainly, many of the heartier soups, pasta, and rice dishes in chapter 3 are enough for a main course if accompanied or followed with a salad or one or more vegetable side dishes.

The food of the poor has always consisted largely of vegetables or beans combined with pasta, potatoes, rice, *polenta*, buckwheat (*polenta taragna*), or some other grain. In addition, from the fourth century, when the Roman Catholic church instituted abstinence from meat during Lent, Advent, Fridays of every week, and certain other days preceding holy days, nonmeat dishes have been the subsistence and tradition of Italian cooks. Elaborate dinners of many courses were forbidden by papal decree during these days of abstinence, which total to nearly one third of the year. Self-denial has never been a characteristic of the exuberant Italian peoples, however. To get around the sumptuary laws, one-pot dishes were devised that incorporated a great variety of foods. Thus even penitential menus were artfully devised and rich in flavor. The tradition of these main course vegetarian dishes continues, even though in recent years the church has abolished its requirements of abstinence from meat.

*Uova Affogate* (Poached Eggs in Tomato Sauce) →

# UOVA AFFOGATE

❈

POACHED EGGS IN TOMATO SAUCE

FOR 2 PEOPLE

**H**ERE IS A DISH I VIVIDLY REMEMBER FROM MY CHILDHOOD. IT WAS OFTEN SERVED WHEN THERE WAS NOTHING ELSE IN THE HOUSE FOR LUNCH, AND MY MOTHER HAD TO WHIP SOMETHING UP. IT IS A DELICIOUS TREATMENT OF EGGS, AND NOT ONE THAT SHOULD BE RELEGATED TO THE "WHEN THERE ISN'T ANYTHING ELSE" STATUS. **BRUSCHETTA** IS THE PERFECT THING FOR MOPPING UP THE SAUCE THAT REMAINS.

Pass the tomatoes and their purée through a food mill or a sieve. Set aside.

Select a skillet large enough to accommodate the eggs later. Combine the olive oil, garlic, and onion in the cold skillet and place over low heat. Stir, cover, and then cook gently until the garlic and onion are wilted, about 3 minutes. Add the tomato paste and stir in. Now stir in the sieved tomatoes, basil, and salt and pepper to taste. Simmer gently uncovered, stirring occasionally, for about 20 minutes. The sauce should be thick, not watery. If the sauce is thin, simmer uncovered for a little longer.

Now proceed in one of two ways: Crack each of the eggs in a cup or small bowl first, to be sure the yolk is intact, and slip each directly into the simmering sauce. Try to do this quickly so the eggs will all go in at about the same time. Immediately cover the pan and continue to simmer gently 2 or 3 minutes, or until a white skin forms over the yolks. Be sure not to overcook the eggs, or the yolks will be hard. Transfer the eggs and the sauce to indivudual plates. Alternatively, first poach the eggs in an egg poacher, then cover them with the sauce when you have transferred them to individual plates.

Serve the eggs immediately with the *bruschetta*.

*1 can (28 ounces) plum tomatoes in*
  *purée*
*2 tablespoons extra-virgin olive oil*
*1 large clove garlic, finely chopped*
*1 small onion, finely chopped*
*2 tablespoons tomato paste*
*several leaves of fresh basil, coarsley*
  *chopped*
*salt*
*freshly milled black or white pepper*
*4 eggs, as fresh as possible*
bruschetta semplice *(page 48) for*
  *two people*

# OMELETTE RIPIENE ALLA BESCIAMELLA

✿

BAKED STUFFED OMELETS WITH BÉCHAMEL, MUSHROOMS, AND PEAS

FOR 6 PEOPLE

ANOTHER FAMILY RECIPE FOR EGGS. MY MOTHER SOMETIMES MADE THESE STUFFED OMELETS FOR LUNCH WHEN WE HAD LEFTOVER **BÉCHAMEL** SAUCE, BUT THEY ARE DELICIOUS ENOUGH TO BE WORTHY OF MAKING FOR THEIR OWN SAKE. THE **BÉCHAMEL** SHOULD BE VERY THICK, AND NOT AT ALL RUNNY, THEREFORE MORE FLOUR AND LESS MILK IS USED. THE NUTTY FLAVOR OF **GROVIERA** OR FRENCH **GRUYÈRE** IS A FOIL FOR THE CREAMY, MILD **BÉCHAMEL** IN THE FILLING, AND MELTS NICELY WITHOUT BECOMING OILY.

Make the tomato sauce. While it is cooking, make the *béchamel* sauce. Pour the milk into a saucepan and place over medium heat until scalded. Meanwhile, in a thick-bottomed saucepan over medium-low heat, melt the butter. Add the flour and stir with a wooden spoon to smooth out any lumps. Over low heat, allow the flour-butter paste to bubble gently while stirring continuously for about 2 minutes. Add the heated milk, 1 tablespoon at a time, continuing to stir. Continue to add the hot milk very slowly, now several tablespoons at a time. If you are not an old hand at this, remove from the heat as you add the milk, stirring all the time. If lumps start to appear, you are probably adding the milk too quickly or in quantities that are too large, or the heat may be too high. To correct lumps, turn off the heat and stir, pressing them against the side of the pan. Continue to add the hot milk very gradually. When all the milk has been added, simmer the sauce over low heat until it is thick and creamy, about 15 minutes, stirring all the time. The sauce should be very thick and not at all runny. Add the salt, pepper to taste, and nutmeg during the last 10 to 15 minutes of cooking.

To make the filling, use a soft brush or clean kitchen towel to remove any dirt from the mushrooms. Do not wash them because water alters their texture. Trim off the tough bottoms from the stems and discard. Slice the mushrooms thinly.

In a skillet over medium heat large enough to accommodate the mushrooms later, melt the 2 tablespoons butter with the olive oil over medium heat. Add the green onions and sauté gently until softened, about 7 minutes. Add the mush-

*½ recipe tomato sauce for Eggplant Parmigiana, Method 2 (page 103), or 1 cup favorite homemade tomato sauce*

*For the* béchamel *sauce:*
*1-¼ cups milk*
*3 tablespoons unsalted butter*
*3 tablespoons all-purpose flour*
*¼ teaspoon salt*
*freshly milled white pepper*
*⅛ teaspoon freshly grated nutmeg*

*For the mushroom filling:*
*10 ounces fresh cultivated mushrooms*
*2 tablespoons unsalted butter*
*1 tablespoon olive oil*
*2 green onions, including 2 inches of the green tops, thinly sliced*
*1 tablespoon chopped fresh Italian parsley*

¼ teaspoon salt

freshly milled black pepper


For the omelets:

scant 5 tablespoons all-purpose flour

½ cup milk

7 extra-large eggs

½ teaspoon salt

freshly milled white pepper

2 tablespoons freshly grated parmigiano

2 tablespoons vegetable oil or unsalted
   butter


¾ cup shredded groviera or French
   gruyère

1 tablespoon freshly grated parmigiano

6 ounces fresh or frozen shelled peas,
   half-cooked

rooms and sauté until the mushrooms are tender, about 8 minutes. Stir in the parsley. Add the salt and pepper to taste. Set aside.

Preheat an oven to 375 degrees F.

To make the omelets, in a bowl, first make a paste with the flour and milk. Beat in the eggs, salt, pepper to taste, and the 2 tablespoons *parmigiano*. Heat 1 teaspoon of the vegetable oil or butter in a 6-inch omelet pan, preferably non-stick. Measure ¼ cup of the egg mixture and pour it into the pan. Tilt the pan to cover the bottom evenly and cook over gentle heat until the top is firm but not dry, about 1 minute total. Turn it out onto a sheet of waxed paper on a plate or counter. Cook the remaining egg mixture in this same manner, always adding a little more of the oil or butter to the pan first, until all the egg mixture is used up. Allow the omelets to cool; you should have 12 to 14 omelets in all.

Lightly grease an 11-by-14-inch baking pan. Smear a generous tablespoonful of the *béchamel* over the surface of each omelet, avoiding the edges. Then place a spoonful of the mushroom mixture in one corner of the disk; sprinkle with some of the *groviera*. Starting from the edge where the mushrooms are, roll up the omelets and place them, seam side down, in the baking pan. Spoon the tomato sauce over the omelet rolls. Sprinkle with the 1 tablespoon *parmigiano* and the peas.

Cover with aluminum foil and bake until the sauce is bubbly and the omelet rolls are heated through, about 15 minutes. Allow to settle for 5 minutes, then, using a spatula, serve the omelet rolls directly from the baking pan. Serve hot.

# FRITTATE

❀

## ITALIAN OMELETS

A SIMPLE, RUSTIC DISH, THE **FRITTATA** NEVERTHELESS HAS MANY VARIATIONS, BOTH SWEET AND SAVORY. INGREDIENTS THAT CAN BE INCORPORATED INCLUDE ALMOST EVERY CONCEIVABLE CATEGORY OF FOOD. IT IS A PARTICULARLY ADAPTABLE VEGETARIAN DISH, AS IT MIGHT INCLUDE ANYTHING FROM PASTA AND RICE TO LITERALLY ANY VEGETABLE, NUT, OR HERB. SWEET **FRITTATE** MIGHT INCLUDE CANDIED FRUITS, RAISINS, OR FRESH FRUITS, ALTHOUGH THEY WOULD TYPICALLY BE SERVED AS A DESSERT COURSE. ❀ THE ITALIAN **FRITTATA**—LITERALLY, "FRIED DISH"— IS NOT A BUTTER-CODDLED OMELET. IT IS A KIND OF **SFORMATO**, OR "MOLD," OF EGGS AND OTHER INGREDIENTS. **FRITTATE** ARE FIRM NOT RUNNY, AND WHEN TURNED OUT OF THE PAN, THEY RESEMBLE A LOW, FLAT CAKE RATHER THAN THE PUFFY CRESCENT OF THE CLASSIC FRENCH OMELET. UNLIKE AN OMELET, WHICH IS FLAVORED WITH HERBS OR WHAT HAVE YOU BUT NOT DOMINATED BY THEM, THE FILLING IN A **FRITTATA** IS AT LEAST AS IMPORTANT AS THE EGGS. ❀ WHEN I WAS GROWING UP, MY MOTHER USED TO REMINISCE ABOUT A PEA **FRITTATA** SHE OFTEN ATE WHEN SHE WAS A YOUNG WOMAN LIVING IN ROME, BUT SHE ALWAYS INSISTED IT COULDN'T BE DUPLICATED IN AMERICA WITH FROZEN PEAS (FRESH-PICKED PEAS BEING IMPOSSIBLE TO FIND IN ROCKLAND COUNTY, NEW YORK, WHEN I WAS A CHILD, AND HOME-GROWN PEAS SOMEHOW NEVER FLOURISHING IN OUR GARDEN). I SHAMEFULLY ADMIT NOW THAT I WAS EMBARRASSED BY MY MOTHER'S EGGY DELIGHTS WHEN THEY APPEARED IN MY SCHOOL LUNCHBOX BETWEEN TWO SLICES OF BREAD—A COMMON WAY OF EATING **FRITTATE**. HOW DID ONE EXPLAIN TO AMERICAN SCHOOLMATES WHAT A **FRITTATA** WAS AND WHY IT WAS BETWEEN TWO SLICES OF BREAD? AT THE PROMPTING OF HER CHILDREN, MY MOTHER EVENTUALLY BECAME AMERICANIZED IN THE MATTER OF SCHOOL LUNCHES AND **FRITTATE** DISAPPEARED FROM OUR SANDWICHES. (I AM HAPPY TO SAY THAT I SURVIVED THE RITUALS OF ADOLESCENCE, WITH ITS RIGID RULES OF CONFORMITY, WITH AN APPRECIATION OF **FRITTATA** SANDWICHES INTACT.) BUT **FRITTATE** REMAINED A RITUAL OF SUPPER, WHICH IN THE ITALIAN HOUSEHOLD IS USUALLY A LIGHT AFFAIR.

# FRITTATA DI PEPERONI
# E CIPOLLE

❋

RED PEPPER AND ONION FRITTATA

FOR 6 PEOPLE

**T**HIS IS A PARTICULARLY COLORFUL **FRITTATA**. THE RED AND YELLOW BELL PEPPERS CREATE A COLORFUL TERRAZZO EFFECT. THE COMBINATION OF PEPPERS AND ONIONS MAKE THIS **FRITTATA** STARTLINGLY SWEET. A SALAD OF MIXED GREENS WITH A VINEGAR AND OIL DRESSING OFFSETS IT BEAUTIFULLY.

6 large bell peppers, a mixture of red
    and yellow

¼ cup plus 1-½ tablespoons extra-
    virgin olive oil

1 extra-large or 2 medium-sized onions,
    quartered and thinly sliced

9 eggs

2 tablespoons chopped fresh Italian
    parsley

3 tablespoons freshly grated parmigiano

2 teaspoons salt

plenty of freshly milled white or black
    pepper

Cut the peppers in half and remove and discard the ribs, seeds, and stems. Cut them into strips about 2 inches long and ½ inch wide. Set aside.

In a flameproof, nonstick 12-inch omelet pan or skillet over medium-low heat, warm the ¼ cup olive oil. Add the onion and sauté until wilted, about 8 minutes. Using a slotted spoon, transfer the onion to a dish and set aside. Be sure to drain any oil in the dish back into the pan.

Warm the oil again over medium-low heat. Add the bell peppers and sauté gently until soft, 15 to 20 minutes, tossing occasionally to cook them evenly.

Meanwhile, in a bowl, beat the eggs lightly with a fork. Stir in the parsley, cheese, salt, and pepper.

When the peppers are cooked, combine them with the onion. When it has cooled enough not to cook the eggs, stir the pepper and onion mixture into the egg mixture.

Preheat a broiler. Wipe the pan clean and pour the 1-½ tablespoons oil into it. Use a pastry brush to oil the sides of the pan as well as the bottom to insure that the *frittata* will not stick to the pan when you unmold it. Place the pan over medium heat. When it is hot enough to make the eggs sizzle, add the egg mixture, using a fork or spoon to distribute the vegetables evenly. Immediately reduce the heat to low and cook until the *frittata* is set but not browned, 12 to 15 minutes. Take care not to overcook the eggs or they will lose their delicacy.

To finish cooking, slide the pan under the preheated broiler 6 inches from the heat. Broil until the top is golden, 1 to 2 minutes. Using a spatula, loosen the edges from the pan and slide the *frittata* out onto a serving plate. Serve warm or at room temperature, cut into wedges.

# TORTINO DI ZUCCHINI GIALLI
# COI FUNGHI

✹

YELLOW SQUASH AND MUSHROOM FLAN

FOR 4 TO 6 PEOPLE

THE LITERAL TRANSLATION OF **TORTINO** IS "LITTLE CAKE." THE MAIN DIFFERENCE BETWEEN A **TORTINO** AND A **FRITTATA** IS THAT THE FORMER IS BAKED IN THE OVEN, WHILE THE LATTER IS COOKED IN A SKILLET ON THE STOVE TOP. CREAM, FLOUR, OR EVEN BREAD CRUMBS ARE SOMETIMES ADDED TO A **TORTINO**, GIVING IT A MORE CAKELIKE TEXTURE. LIKE A **FRITTATA**, A **TORTINO** CAN BE MADE WITH ALMOST ANYTHING, INCLUDING CHEESES, VEGETABLES OF ALL KINDS, AND EVEN FRUIT.

Preheat an oven to 400 degrees F. Wash the squashes well to remove any imbedded dirt. Trim off the stems and navels. Cut the squashes in half lengthwise, then cut crosswise into thin half-moon slices. Set aside.

Use a soft brush or clean kitchen towel to remove any dirt from the mushrooms. Do not wash them because water alters their texture. Trim off the tough bottoms from the stems and discard. Slice the mushrooms thinly. Set aside.

In a skillet over medium-low heat, melt the 2 tablespoons butter. Add the onion and sauté gently until softened, about 6 minutes. Add the mushrooms and continue to sauté until they are tender, about 4 minutes. Add the sliced squash and the mint and toss to coat with the butter. Sauté, uncovered, for 5 minutes, stirring after 3 minutes. Cover the pan and continue to cook over low heat until tender, about 10 minutes. Pour the contents of the skillet into a colander to drain off excess liquid.

In a large bowl, beat the eggs lightly. Beat in the *parmigiano, fontina,* salt, and pepper. When the drained squash has cooled enough not to cook the eggs, stir it into the egg mixture, mixing well. Butter an 8-by-11-inch baking dish. Pour in the egg-and-squash mixture. Use a fork to distribute the vegetables evenly in the dish. Sprinkle with the crumbs and place on the middle rack in the oven.

Bake until set, about 20 minutes. Remove from the oven and allow to settle for 10 minutes before cutting. Serve warm or at room temperature.

AHEAD-OF-TIME NOTE: The *tortino* can be baked up to 2 days in advance, cooled, and refrigerated. Bring it to room temperature before serving.

*1 pound young, firm yellow summer squashes (each weighing between 6 and 8 ounces)*

*½ pound fresh cultivated mushrooms*

*2 tablespoons unsalted butter, plus additional butter for greasing the baking pan*

*1 onion, chopped*

*1 tablespoon chopped fresh mint*

*4 extra-large eggs*

*2 tablespoons freshly grated parmigiano*

*¼ pound fontina, cut into small dice*

*¾ teaspoon salt*

*⅛ teaspoon freshly milled white pepper*

*1 teaspoon fine dried bread crumbs*

# PASTICCIO DI ZUCCHINI

✻

### BAKED ZUCCHINI CASSEROLE

FOR 6 TO 8 PEOPLE

**A** PASTICCIO—LITERALLY, A "MESS," FIGURATIVELY, A "PIE"—IS A BAKED DISH OF VEGETABLES, PASTA, RICE, OR OTHER THINGS THAT IS BOUND WITH A BATTER OF BEATEN EGGS AND GRATED **PARMIGIANO, BÉCHAMEL** SAUCE, OR CREAM. I CONCOCTED THIS AT MY SISTER-IN-LAW'S FARM ONE AUGUST AFTERNOON WHEN ZUCCHINI WERE IN GREAT ABUNDANCE. I HAVE HAD OTHER VARIATIONS ON THE DISH THAT INCLUDE POTATOES AND EGGPLANT, ALTHOUGH ALMOST ANY VEGETABLE WOULD BE DELICIOUS COOKED THIS WAY. FOR BEST RESULTS, USE THE FRESHEST ZUCCHINI POSSIBLE.

*2 pounds young, firm zucchini (prefer-*
*ably no more than 6 ounces each)*

*4 eggs*

*1 teaspoon salt*

*¼ teaspoon freshly milled black pepper*

*1-½ cups fine dried bread crumbs*

*1 cup freshly grated* parmigiano

*a handful of fresh basil leaves, torn into*
*small pieces (about 3 tablespoons)*

*2 teaspoons chopped fresh thyme, or 1*
*teaspoon dried thyme*

*2 tablespoons chopped fresh Italian*
*parsley*

*extra-virgin olive oil for oiling baking*
*dish and for drizzling*

*1 pound mozzarella, sliced into small,*
*thin pieces*

*1 large or 2 medium-sized vine-ripened*
*tomatoes, thinly sliced*

Preheat an oven to 350 degrees F. Wash the zucchini thoroughly to remove any imbedded dirt. Trim off the stems and navels. Cut the zucchini lengthwise into paper-thin slices. Set aside.

In a bowl beat the eggs lightly. Beat in the salt and pepper and set aside. In a separate bowl stir together the bread crumbs, *parmigiano*, basil, thyme, and parsley. Set this aside as well.

Rub the bottom of an 11-by-14-inch baking dish with a little olive oil. Place a layer of zucchini slices on the bottom. Over that arrange a layer of mozzarella, then a layer of tomato slices. Sprinkle some of the bread crumb mixture over the top and then drizzle lightly with olive oil. Repeat layering until all the vegetables and mozzarella are used up, ending with a layer of mozzarella and drizzling each layer of bread crumbs with oil. Pour the egg mixture evenly over the top.

Bake in the preheated oven until the top is golden and the egg is set, about 45 minutes. If the casserole begins to brown too quickly, place a sheet of aluminum foil, dull side out, over it and remove the foil for the last 5 minutes of baking. Remove from the oven and allow to settle for 10 minutes before cutting. Serve warm, at room temperature, or cold, cut into squares.

# MELANZANE ALLA PARMIGIANA

✸

EGGPLANT PARMIGIANA

FOR 6 PEOPLE

DESPITE THE REFERENCE TO AND USE OF **PARMIGIANO-REGGIANO**, THE FAMOUS CHEESE OF THE NORTHERN REGION OF PARMA, THIS UNIVERSALLY ITALIAN DISH, SOMETIMES REFERRED TO AS **MELANZANE ALLA NAPOLETANA**, ORIGINATED IN NAPLES SOMETIME AFTER THE TOMATO WAS ACCEPTED AS NONPOISONOUS IN THE EIGHTEENTH CENTURY. IN ITALY, EGGPLANT PARMIGIANA MIGHT BE SERVED AS AN **ANTIPASTO**, AS A **PIETANZA** (A COMPLETE MEAL), OR AS A **CONTORNO**. RESTAURANT AND PIZZERIA VERSIONS IN AMERICA ARE SOMETIMES DISAPPOINTING, WITH THE EGGPLANT TOO HEAVY AND GREASY AND THE TOMATO SAUCE UNPLEASANTLY BITTER FROM AN OVERDOSE OF OREGANO (THE ORIGINAL VERSION CONTAINS NO OREGANO) AND FROM OVERCOOKING. THIS HEAVY-HANDEDNESS WITH OREGANO (AUTHENTIC ITALIAN TOMATO SAUCES RARELY, IF EVER, CONTAIN OREGANO) AND COOKING TO DEATH OF TOMATO SAUCE ARE PARTICULARLY COMMON MISTAKES. ✸ **PECORINO**, A SHARPER SHEEP'S MILK CHEESE, MAY HAVE ORIGINALLY BEEN USED IN PLACE OF **PARMIGIANO**. BUT **PARMIGIANO** HAS BECOME A UNIVERSAL CHEESE, AND NO **MELANZANE ALLA PARMIGIANA** WOULD BE THE SAME WITHOUT IT. IN NAPLES, HOWEVER, **CACIOCAVALLO**, ALSO CALLED **SCAMORZA**, A SLIGHTLY AGED, HARD MOZZARELLA, IS SOMETIMES USED IN PLACE OF BUTTERY-SOFT FRESH MOZZARELLA. MANY RECIPES FOR THIS DISH CALL FOR LARGER QUANTITIES OF CHEESES, BUT I FIND THAT TOO MUCH CHEESE DETRACTS. ✸ A VARIATION ON THIS DISH IS TO MAKE IT WITH ZUCCHINI INSTEAD OF EGGPLANT. SELECT SMALL OR MEDIUM ZUCCHINI, CUTTING AND COOKING THEM JUST AS YOU WOULD EGGPLANT. ZUCCHINI, HOWEVER, REQUIRE NO SALTING PRIOR TO COOKING. ✸ A GOOD EGGPLANT PARMIGIANA CAN BE MADE BY BROILING OR GRILLING THE EGGPLANT SLICES RATHER THAN FRYING THEM. IT PRODUCES A LIGHTER DISH THAN THE FRYING METHOD. FOR BEST RESULTS, HOWEVER, THE EGGPLANT SHOULD BE BAKED IN A SINGLE LAYER. THIS MEANS THAT YOU MUST HAVE SIX BAKING DISHES, EACH APPROXIMATELY EIGHT BY TWELVE INCHES, FOR THREE POUNDS OF EGGPLANT. THE PROCEDURE FOLLOWS IN METHOD **2**.

METHOD 1 Cut the stems and navels off the eggplants and cut them crosswise into rounds ¼ inch thick. Sprinkle each slice lightly with salt. Place the rounds in a colander, standing them upright so the bitter liquid from the seeds drains off easily, about 40 minutes.

Meanwhile, to make the sauce, put the tomatoes in a saucepan. Cook uncovered over gentle heat, stirring occasionally, until thickened, about 40 minutes. If

*3 eggplants (about 3 pounds total weight)*
*salt*

*For the tomato sauce:*
*2-½ pounds very ripe, vine-ripened*
*    plum tomatoes, cut into quarters;*

*1 can (28 ounces) plum tomatoes in
purée, roughly chopped; or 2 cans
(28 ounces) plum tomatoes, drained
and roughly chopped*

*¼ teaspoon salt, or to taste*

*freshly milled white or black pepper*

*1 cup all-purpose flour for dredging*

*salt*

*freshly milled white or black pepper*

*safflower oil for frying*

*unsalted butter for greasing baking dish*

*lightly toasted fine dried bread crumbs
for coating baking dish (page 17)*

*¼ cup chopped fresh basil*

*1 pound fresh mozzarella, thinly sliced
or shredded*

*½ cup freshly grated* parmigiano

you see that the tomatoes give off a great deal of water, drain off excess liquid as they cook. Remove from the heat and let cool slightly, then pass the tomatoes through a food mill, using the attachment with the largest holes to get a smooth purée and pressing to get as much of the pulp as you can through the holes. If the purée is too thin to be a good sauce consistency (this will depend upon the texture and water content of the tomatoes), return it to a saucepan and simmer gently for up to 20 minutes longer. Season with the salt and pepper to taste.

Place a large sheet of waxed paper on the kitchen counter. Pour the flour into it and then season the flour with salt and pepper to taste.

Use a clean kitchen towel or paper towels to blot the salt and sweat from the eggplant. In a skillet over medium-high heat, pour in oil to a depth of 1 inch. Heat the oil until it is hot enough to make the eggplant sizzle. As soon as the oil is hot enough, but not before, dredge several eggplant slices in the flour, shake off the excess flour, and slip them into the hot oil. Fry on both sides, turning once, until tender and golden, about 8 minutes total cooking time. Remove to paper towels to drain well. Fry the remaining slices, dredging them only when you are ready to fry them.

Preheat an oven to 400 degrees F. Butter a 10-by-14-inch baking dish and coat it with the crumbs, shaking out any excess. (A smaller baking dish will do just fine, but it will result in a smaller casserole with a greater number of layers. I prefer to use a dish that will result in fewer layers.) Before placing each slice of eggplant in the dish, blot it with fresh paper towels once. Place a layer of eggplant in the dish, a little of the sauce, some of the chopped basil, then a layer of mozzarella, and finally a sprinkling of *parmigiano*. Continue layering the ingredients in this order, ending with a layer of eggplant smeared with sauce and sprinkled with *parmigiano* and the remaining basil (the green of the basil makes the dish exceptionally pretty).

Cover the baking dish loosely with aluminum foil and slide it onto the top rack of the oven. Bake until bubbly, about 20 minutes. Remove from the oven and allow to settle for 10 minutes before serving. Serve hot or at room temperature.

AHEAD-OF-TIME NOTE: The sauce can be made 2 or 3 days in advance. Although the dish is best when freshly made, it can be assembled and refrigerated the day before, and then baked before serving. Alternatively, bake the dish a day in advance, cover and refrigerate; the next day reheat in a preheated 400 degree F oven for about 20 minutes.

METHOD 2 Slice, salt, and blot the eggplants as directed in Method 1.

Meanwhile, make the sauce. In a saucepan over medium heat, warm the olive oil. Add the onion and sauté gently until softened, 7 to 8 minutes. Add the tomatoes, salt, and pepper to taste, and stir well. Cover partially and simmer over medium-low heat until a thick sauce forms, about 1 hour. Stir occasionally. If the tomatoes contain a great deal of water, it may be necessary to pour off excess liquid.

Preheat a gas or electric grill or broiler, or prepare a fire in a charcoal grill. Brush the eggplant slices on both sides with the oil. If using an indoor or outdoor grill, cook the slices, turning once, until they are lightly colored on both sides; do not char them. If using a broiler, place the eggplant slices on baking sheets about 6 inches from the heat. Broil, turning once, until lightly colored, a total of 5 or 6 minutes.

Preheat an oven to 325 degrees F. Dip the eggplant slices in the crumbs and arrange them in a single layer in 6 baking dishes each measuring 8 by 12 inches. Using a spoon smear each slice with some of the sauce, then sprinkle with basil, top with mozzarella, and sprinkle with *parmigiano*.

Bake, uncovered, until the cheese melts and is lightly golden, about 15 minutes. Serve hot or at room temperature.

*3 eggplants (about 3 pounds total weight)*

*For the tomato sauce:*
*2 tablespoons extra-virgin olive oil*
*1 onion, finely chopped*
*2-½ pounds vine-ripened plum tomatoes, peeled, seeded, and finely chopped, or 1 can (28 ounces) plum tomatoes in their own juices, drained, seeded, and chopped*
*½ teaspoon salt*
*freshly milled white or black pepper*

*5 tablespoons extra-virgin olive oil*

*¾ cup fine dried bread crumbs, lightly toasted (page 17)*
*¼ cup chopped fresh basil*
*½ pound mozzarella, finely sliced or shredded*
*¾ cup freshly grated* parmigiano

# POLENTA

✶

BASIC POLENTA

FOR 6 PEOPLE

**I**F YOU CANNOT FIND IMPORTED ITALIAN CORNMEAL FOR **POLENTA**, A FINE SUBSTITUTE IS GOYA BRAND GROUND CORNMEAL.  GOYA CORNMEAL COMES IN FINE AND COARSE GRIND.  A GOOD TEXTURE FOR **POLENTA** CAN BE MADE FROM A COMBINATION OF THE TWO IN EQUAL PARTS.  THERE IS AN IMPORTED ITALIAN INSTANT **POLENTA** THAT COOKS IN FIVE MINUTES, BUT IT IS EXPENSIVE AND THICKENS AND COOKS SO QUICKLY THAT LUMPS EASILY FORM BEFORE THE **POLENTA** CAN BE STIRRED PROPERLY.

*7 cups water*
*1 tablespoon salt*
*2 cups coarse cornmeal*
*additional boiling water if necessary*
*unsalted butter and freshly grated*
  *parmigiano if serving loose*

Bring the water to a boil in a deep pot.  Add the salt.  Then add the cornmeal very slowly, almost in a trickle.  Adding the cornmeal gradually prevents lumps from forming, and will also keep the boiling temperature constant, which is important if the *polenta* is to become properly soft and creamy.  The flame should be set at medium heat so the *polenta* continues to boil.  If the heat is too low, it will simply stew and not cook properly.  From the instant the cornmeal is added to the water, stir it without interruption using a long-handled wooden spoon, always in the same direction.  After all the cornmeal is absorbed, continue to stir constantly until the *polenta* is thick and pulls away easily with the spoon from the sides of the pan.  If the *polenta* is quite thick but still not pulling away easily from the pan, add a little more boiling water and continue to stir until it is ready.  It should be perfectly cooked, thick, and creamy in 25 to 30 minutes.

If you are serving the *polenta* loose, stir in a large lump of butter and sprinkle with grated cheese.  Or pour it onto a large platter, make an indentation in the center with a large metal spoon dipped in hot water, and place a vegetable stew or whatever in the hollow.

If you intend to spread the *polenta* out to cool, lightly oil two pastry boards or baking sheets, or a very large scratchproof counter surface.  Pour the hot *polenta* directly from the pan onto the board or counter.  Use a large knife or rubber spatula, first dipped in water, to spread it out to a thickness of about ½ inch, or whatever the recipe directs.  Allow it to cool and harden, about 20 minutes, before cutting into squares or whatever shape you need.

# POLENTA CON FUNGHI DI BOSCO

✹

## POLENTA WITH WILD MUSHROOMS

FOR 6 PEOPLE

THIS IS A DISH FROM THE VENEZIA-GIULIA REGION. THE FRESH **PORCINI** THAT WOULD BE USED IN THE SAUCE THERE ARE DIFFICULT TO FIND HERE, SO I HAVE REPLACED THEM WITH A COMBINATION OF FRESH **SHIITAKE** AND OYSTER MUSHROOMS, WHICH ARE BOTH QUITE COMMONPLACE IN AMERICAN MARKETS. OTHER VARIETIES OF FRESH WILD MUSHROOMS MAY ALSO BE USED (PAGES 19 AND 21).

Using a soft brush or clean kitchen towel, remove any dirt from the mushrooms. Don't wash them because water alters their texture. Trim off the woody stems. Thinly slice the caps and tender stems. In a skillet over medium heat, melt the butter. Add the onion, garlic, and parsley and sauté until softened, about 4 minutes. Add the mushrooms and sauté over gentle heat, stirring occasionally, for about 5 minutes. Add the broth, salt, and pepper to taste. Cover and cook gently for 5 minutes.

In a small cup stir together the water and flour to form a runny, smooth mixture. Stir it into the skillet with the mushrooms. Re-cover and continue to cook gently, stirring occasionally, until the sauce thickens and the mushrooms are tender, about 10 minutes. (The amount of time required will depend on the amount of moisture in the mushrooms.) Keep the skillet covered, but if the mushrooms appear a little dry (they should form a sauce), stir in a few more tablespoons of broth or water. Taste for seasoning.

Keep the sauce warm over very low heat while you make the *polenta*. Pour the finished *polenta* onto a large platter and, using a large spoon dipped in very hot water, make a deep indentation in the center. Pour the mushroom sauce into the "well" and serve immediately.

NOTE: Dried *porcini* and fresh cultivated mushrooms may be used in place of the suggested mushrooms. Soak 1 ounce dried *porcini* in ¾ cup warm water for 30 minutes. Strain the mushroom soaking liquid through a paper towel, cheesecloth, or a fine sieve. Reduce the broth measure to 1 cup and combine the soaking liquid with the 1 cup broth.

*For the mushrooms:*

*5 ounces fresh* shiitake *mushrooms*

*5 ounces fresh oyster mushrooms*

*5 tablespoons unsalted butter*

*¼ cup chopped onion*

*1 large clove garlic, finely chopped*

*1 tablespoon chopped fresh Italian parsley*

*1-½ cups Vegetable Broth (page 58)*

*½ teaspoon salt*

*freshly milled white or black pepper*

*1 tablespoon flour*

*2 tablespoons water*

*1 recipe Basic Polenta (page 104)*

# POLENTA PASTICCIATA CON SALSA
# DI FUNGHI

❀

BAKED POLENTA CASSEROLE WITH CREAMY MUSHROOM SAUCE AND FONTINA

FOR 6 PEOPLE

I N A **PASTICCIO, POLENTA** FUNCTIONS MUCH THE SAME AS LASAGNE NOODLES DO. THE HARDENED **POLENTA** SQUARES ARE ARRANGED IN ALTERNATING LAYERS WITH THE MUSHROOM SAUCE. WHEN BAKED, THE **POLENTA**, SAUCE, AND CHEESE FUSE INTO A UNIFIED DISH. THE GRAINY TEXTURE OF THE POLENTA IS A DELIGHTFUL CONTRAST TO THE CREAMY MUSHROOM SAUCE. THIS RECIPE IS IN THE NORTHERN TRADITION, WITH ITS USE OF CREAM AND **FONTINA**, THE NUTTY, CREAMY CHEESE OF VALLE D'AOSTA.

*For the sauce:*

*1 ounce dried* porcini

*¾ cup hot water*

*½ pound fresh cultivated white
    mushrooms*

*2 tablespoons unsalted butter*

*1 tablespoon extra-virgin olive oil*

*1 small onion, chopped*

*½ teaspoon salt*

*¼ teaspoon freshly milled white pepper*

*½ cup heavy cream*

*olive oil or vegetable oil for oiling boards
    and baking dish*

*1 recipe Basic* Polenta *(page 104) made
    with 1-½ cups cornmeal, 6 cups
    water, and 2 teaspoons salt*

*½ pound (2 cups) shredded* fontina

*⅓ cup freshly grated* parmigiano

To begin to prepare the sauce, in a small bowl combine the dried *porcini* and hot water and let stand for 45 minutes to 1 hour. Remove the *porcini* and squeeze out excess water. Using scissors, cut them into pieces about the size of your thumbnail. Set aside. Strain the mushroom liquor through a paper towel or a fine sieve; reserve.

Lightly oil an 8-by-11-inch baking pan and set it aside. Lightly oil two large pastry boards or baking sheets, or a very large scratchproof counter surface. Make the *polenta* and when it is cooked, turn it directly out onto the boards, counter, or baking sheets. Use a large knife or rubber spatula, first dipped in cold water, to spread out the *polenta* to a thickness of about ½ inch. Allow it to cool and harden, about 20 minutes. Cut it into approximate 3-inch squares.

Meanwhile, preheat an oven to 400 degrees F. Continue to make the sauce. Using a soft brush or clean kitchen towel, remove any dirt from the fresh mushrooms. Don't wash them because water will alter their texture. Separate the stems from the caps, discarding the stems if they are tough. Slice the mushroom caps and tender stems thinly. In a skillet over medium-low heat, melt the butter with the oil. Add the onion and sauté until softened, about 5 minutes. Add the *porcini* and sauté for another 5 or 6 minutes to marry the flavors. Add the cultivated mushrooms and continue to sauté until tender, about 5 minutes. Add the mushroom soaking liquid, salt, and pepper. Allow to simmer gently for 5 minutes, stirring occasionally. Then stir in the cream, and allow the mix-

ture barely to reach a simmer.  Immediately remove the skillet from the heat.

Place half of the *polenta* squares in a layer on the bottom of the prepared dish. Spread half of the sauce in a layer over them, then sprinkle with half of the cheeses.  Place another layer of *polenta* squares over the cheeses.  Spoon the remaining sauce on top and sprinkle with the remaining cheeses.  Place on the middle rack of the oven and bake until the cheese is melted and golden and the *pasticcio* is bubbling, about 20 minutes.  Remove from the oven and let settle for 10 minutes before cutting into squares.  Serve hot.

AHEAD-OF-TIME NOTE:  This *pasticcio* can be assembled up to 3 days in advance, covered, and refrigerated, and then baked just before serving.  Leftover *pasticcio* reheats well:  Cover with aluminum foil and place in a preheated 375 degree F oven for 20 to 30 minutes, depending on whether it is chilled or at room temperature.

# CÚSCUS SICILIANO-ARABO

❈

COUSCOUS WITH STEWED VEGETABLES AND CHICK-PEAS, SICILIAN-ARAB STYLE

FOR 6 PEOPLE

COUSCOUS APPEARS IN THE TRADITIONAL CUISINES OF BOTH SICILY AND SARDINIA, CLEARLY A LEGACY OF THE SARACEN INFLUENCE IN THOSE ISLANDS. IN SICILY, IT IS CHARACTERISTICALLY COOKED WITH FISH, AND IN SARDINIA WITH LAMB. THE DUCA DI SALAPARUTA, A SICILIAN ARISTOCRAT DEVOTED TO VEGETARIANISM, MENTIONS A SICILIAN RECIPE FOR A VEGETARIAN COUSCOUS IN HIS BOOK, **CUCINA VEGETARIANA E NATURISMO CRUDO**, WHICH WAS KINDLY GIVEN TO ME BY HIS GRANDCHILDREN. CALLED **CÚSCUS DELLE MONACHE**, "COUSCOUS OF THE NUNS," THE DISH IS COMPRISED OF HOMEMADE COUSCOUS STEAMED OVER VEGETABLE BROTH, COMBINED WITH COOKED VEGETABLES OF THE SEASON. I HAVE DEVISED THIS RECIPE INSPIRED BY SALAPARUTA'S DESCRIPTIONS OF THE SICILIAN DISH, USING A VARIETY OF VEGETABLES I FIND PARTICULARLY HARMONIOUS RATHER THAN THOSE HE RECALLS, WHICH INCLUDE SWEET PEPPERS. I ALSO ADD SHARPLY FLAVORED GREEN OLIVES, WHICH REALLY LIFT THE DISH AND SET OFF THE SWEETNESS OF THE VEGETABLES NICELY. ❈ AS FOR THE COUSCOUS, ASSUMING THAT MOST READERS DO NOT OWN A **COUSCOUSIÈRE**, I PRESCRIBE A SIMPLE AND FOOLPROOF COOKING METHOD THAT PRODUCES PERFECTLY FLUFFY COUSCOUS EVERY TIME. THIS MEANS THAT THE COUSCOUS IS NOT STEAMED OVER THE BROTH, AS IT IS WHEN DONE IN THE TRADITIONAL WAY, BUT THE RESULTS ARE EXCELLENT. CERTAINLY, A GOOD (BOILING HOT) VEGETABLE BROTH LIKE THE ONE ON PAGE 58 CAN REPLACE THE BOILING WATER CALLED FOR IN THE RECIPE.

Peel the eggplant and cut into 1-inch cubes. Place the eggplant cubes in a colander and sprinkle with salt. Place the colander in the sink or over a dish and let stand so the bitter liquid drains out of the seeds, 30 to 40 minutes. Rinse under cold water and pat dry thoroughly with a clean kitchen towel.

In a Dutch oven over medium-low heat, warm the olive oil. Add the onion, garlic, and eggplant and sauté until the eggplant is tender, about 10 minutes.

Meanwhile, in a saucepan bring enough salted water to a boil to cover the cabbage and carrots. Add the cabbage and carrots and parboil for 5 minutes. Remove the cabbage and carrots with a slotted spoon and set the cabbage aside.

To the eggplant mixture in the Dutch oven, add the carrots, fennel, zucchini, green beans, rutabaga, cauliflower, potato, olives, basil, and marjoram. Stir in 1-½ cups of the broth and cover partially. Cook over gentle heat for 15 minutes,

*1 small eggplant*
*salt for sprinkling on eggplant, plus*
    *¾ teaspoon salt*
*¼ cup extra-virgin olive oil*
*1 large onion, coarsely chopped*
*1 large clove garlic, chopped*
*¼ head small green cabbage, cut into*
    *wedges*
*2 carrots, scraped and cut into ½-inch*
    *dice*
*1 medium bulb fennel, stalks and fronds*
    *removed, cut into 6 wedges*

stirring occasionally. Add the chick-peas, salt, and pepper. Cook for an additional 5 minutes. Add the cabbage and the remaining ½ cup broth. Stir, then taste and adjust for seasonings. When heated through, after 3 to 4 minutes, remove from the heat.

During the last 15 minutes that the vegetable stew is cooking, make the couscous. Preheat an oven to 200 degrees F. In a baking dish measuring approximately 9 by 12 inches, pour in the couscous in an even layer. In a bowl or pitcher, combine the boiling water, butter, and the ¾ teaspoon salt, then pour the mixture over the couscous in the baking dish. Stir once with a fork. Cover tightly with aluminum foil and place in the oven for 10 minutes.

Arrange the couscous on a platter and spoon the vegetable stew over it. Serve at once.

1 small zucchini, cut into 1-inch dice

¼ pound green beans, cut into 1-inch pieces

½ large rutabaga, peeled and cut into 1-inch cubes

½ cauliflower, divided into small florets (about 2 cups)

1 large potato, peeled and cut into 1-inch cubes

20 sharply flavored imported green olives, pitted

1 teaspoon chopped fresh basil, or ½ teaspoon dried basil

1 teaspoon chopped fresh marjoram, or ½ teaspoon dried marjoram

2 cups Vegetable Broth (page 58)

3 cups drained, cooked chick-peas

2 teaspoons salt

¼ teaspoon freshly milled black pepper

1-½ cups (10 ounces) couscous

2-¼ cups water, boiling

2 tablespoons unsalted butter

# PASTICCIO DI MELANZANE CON LASAGNE

✱

EGGPLANT AND LASAGNE CASSEROLE

FOR 6 PEOPLE

HERE IS AN INTERESTING VARIATION ON THE CLASSIC EGGPLANT PARMIGIANA (PAGE 101.) WHILE EGGPLANT IS MOST FLAVORFUL WHEN DEEP-FRIED, AS HERE, THE DISH CAN ALSO BE MADE BY GRILLING OR BROILING THE EGGPLANT FIRST (SEE NOTE).

2 eggplants (about 2 pounds total
      weight)
salt

For the sauce:
1 can (28 ounces) plum tomatoes in
      purée
½ pound fresh cultivated mushrooms
2 tablespoons olive oil or extra-virgin
      olive oil
1 large clove garlic, chopped
1 small onion, chopped
1 small carrot, scraped and chopped
2 teaspoons fresh chopped basil, or
      1 teaspoon dried basil
½ teaspoon salt

olive oil or vegetable oil for deep-frying
3-½ quarts water
6 ounces dried lasagne (9 whole
      lasagne noodles)
1 tablespoon salt
½ pound mozzarella, shredded

Trim the stems and navels off the eggplants and cut them crosswise into rounds ¼ inch thick. Sprinkle each slice lightly with salt. Place the rounds in a colander, standing them upright so the bitter liquid drains out of the seeds, about 40 minutes. Use a clean kitchen towel or paper towels to blot the salt and sweat from the eggplants.

Meanwhile, to make the sauce, cut the tomatoes in half crosswise and remove excess seeds by pushing them out with your thumb. Chop the tomatoes. Sieve the tomato purée to remove any seeds. Combine the tomatoes and purée and set aside.

Using a soft brush or clean kitchen towel, remove any dirt from the mushrooms. Don't wash them because water alters their texture. Separate the stems from the caps, discarding the stems if they are tough. Thinly slice the caps and tender stems. In a skillet over medium heat, warm the olive oil. Add the garlic, onion, and carrot and sauté gently, stirring occasionally, until the vegetables are softened, about 12 minutes. Add the mushrooms and sauté gently, stirring now and then, until they are tender, about 5 minutes. Add the tomatoes, purée, basil, and salt. Simmer the sauce gently for 20 minutes.

While the sauce is cooking, in a skillet over medium-high heat, pour in olive oil to a depth of 1 inch. Heat the oil hot enough to make the eggplant sizzle. As soon as the oil is hot enough, but not before, slip the rounds into the hot oil. Fry on both sides, turning once, until they color, about 4 minutes on each side. Remove to paper towels to drain well.

Meanwhile, bring the water to a rolling boil in a large pot. Add the lasagne and salt. Cook over high heat to maintain the boil, stirring frequently, until the noodles are not quite al dente (slightly undercooked), about 10 minutes. Drain the noodles and rinse them in cold water; drain thoroughly again and set aside flat on a sheet of waxed paper.

Preheat an oven to 400 degrees F.

To assemble the *pasticcio*, select a 9-by-12-inch baking dish. Smear the bottom of it with a tablespoon or two of the sauce. In a bowl combine the mozzarella and *pecorino*. Place half of the eggplant rounds in a layer over the sauce. Smear the rounds with a thin layer of the sauce. Then sprinkle with about one fourth of the cheeses. Place a single layer of *lasagne* noodles atop the cheeses, being sure that they are close together and side to side, not on top of one another. Spread a layer of sauce over the noodles, then sprinkle with one third of the remaining cheeses. Arrange the remaining eggplant over that, then again, the sauce, cheese, *lasagne*, sauce, and cheese. To make the topping, in a bowl stir together the eggs, milk, and *parmigiano*. Pour it evenly over the *pasticcio*.

Bake on the middle rack of the oven until the top is golden and the *pasticcio* is bubbling, about 20 minutes. Remove from the oven and allow to settle for 10 minutes before cutting into squares. Serve hot.

AHEAD-OF-TIME NOTE: This *pasticcio* can be assembled up to 3 days in advance, covered, and refrigerated. Leftover *pasticcio* reheats well: Cover with aluminum foil and place in a preheated 375 degree F oven for 20 to 30 minutes, depending upon whether it is chilled or at room temperature.

NOTE: To broil or grill the eggplant, cut, salt, drain, rinse, and dry the eggplants as directed. Brush the eggplant slices generously with olive oil on one side. Place them on an oiled grill rack, or on a baking sheet if you are broiling, oiled side up. Position the grill rack or broiler pan 6 to 8 inches from the heat source; it must not be too close or the eggplant will burn. Grill or broil on both sides, using a metal spatula to flip them, until tender and golden brown. Turn the eggplant slices only once and brush them on the second side with oil as soon as they are turned. Proceed with the recipe.

*¼ pound aged or young* pecorino
  *cheese, grated or shredded, or 1 cup*
  *freshly grated* parmigiano

*For the topping:*
*2 extra-large eggs, lightly beaten*
*2 tablespoons milk or heavy cream*
*2 tablespoons freshly grated* parmigiano

# MACCHERONI CON CAVOLO E FORMAGGIO AL FORNO

⊛

BAKED MACARONI WITH CABBAGE AND CHEESE

FOR 4 TO 6 PEOPLE

HERE IS ONE OF MY MOTHER'S IMPROVISATIONAL RECIPES, ESPECIALLY GOOD ON A COLD WINTER DAY, BUT LIGHT ENOUGH FOR SUMMER DINING AS WELL.

*3 tablespoons olive oil*

*1 large onion, cut into quarters and then thinly sliced*

*1-½ pounds green cabbage, finely shredded*

*1 teaspoon caraway seeds*

*1 tablespoon red wine vinegar*

*½ cup tomato sauce*

*2 tablespoons plus 5 quarts water*

*½ pound elbow macaroni*

*1-½ tablespoons salt, plus salt to taste*

*freshly milled black pepper*

*butter for greasing baking dish*

*½ pound fontina or mozzarella, thinly sliced or shredded*

Preheat an oven to 400 degrees F. In a large skillet over medium-low heat, warm the olive oil. Add the onion and sauté gently until softened, about 5 minutes. Add the cabbage and stir well. Cover and continue to cook over medium-low heat, stirring occasionally, until the cabbage is softened, about 10 minutes. Add the caraway seeds and vinegar and stir to mix. Stir in the tomato sauce and the 2 tablespoons water, cover partially, and cook for an additional 10 minutes. Remove from the heat.

While the cabbage is cooking, bring the 5 quarts water to a rolling boil in a large pot. Add the pasta and the 1-½ tablespoons salt. Stir immediately and continue to cook over high heat, stirring occasionally to prevent the macaroni from sticking together. When the macaroni is not quite *al dente* (slightly undercooked), after about 10 minutes, drain it in a colander and add it to the skillet holding the cabbage. Toss well, then taste for salt and add pepper to taste.

Butter a baking dish measuring approximately 9 by 12 inches. Pour the cabbage and pasta mixture into the dish. Top with the cheese. Cover with aluminum foil and bake for 15 minutes. Uncover and bake for another few minutes. Remove from the oven and serve immediately.

AHEAD-OF-TIME NOTE: The entire casserole can be assembled up to 2 days in advance, covered, and refrigerated. If chilled, add 5 to 10 minutes to the baking time.

# FAGIOLI IN SALSA

✦

## BEANS SIMMERED WITH TOMATO SAUCE

FOR 2 OR 3 PEOPLE

I F PASTA HAS BEEN THE STAFF OF LIFE IN MANY PARTS OF ITALY, BEANS HAVE BEEN AN EQUALLY UBIQUITOUS AND FAR MORE ANCIENT ELEMENT OF THE **CUCINA POVERA**. IN 1895, COOKBOOK AUTHOR PELLEGRINO ARTUSI, WROTE, "WHEN THE WORKER . . . CAN'T EVEN BUY A PIECE OF MEAT TO MAKE A GOOD SOUP FOR HIS LITTLE FAMILY, HE FINDS IN BEANS A HEALING FOOD, NUTRITIOUS AND ECONOMICAL." TODAY, MANY VEGETARIANS FIND VIRTUE IN BEANS FOR MUCH THE SAME REASONS. ✦ THIS RECIPE IS SUITABLE AS AN **ANTIPASTO**, MAIN COURSE, OR SIDE DISH, BUT THE QUANTITY IS FOR MAIN-COURSE PORTIONS. SUITABLE ACCOMPANYING SIDE DISHES WOULD INCLUDE FRIED BABY ARTI-CHOKES (PAGE 31), STUFFED EGGPLANT, BASILICATA STYLE (PAGE 39), STUFFED ZUCCHINI, LIGURIA STYLE (PAGE 40), AND BROCCOLI WITH LEMON AND OLIVE OIL (PAGE 143).

If using dried beans, rinse them and pick them over and then rehydrate and cook them according to the directions on page 15, adding 2 of the bay leaves to the beans while they cook. When the beans are ready, drain them, reserving 1 table-spoon of the liquid. You will have about 3 cups cooked beans. If using drained, canned beans, rinse them and drain well. In both cases, set the beans and the reserved liquid aside.

In a skillet over medium-low heat, warm the olive oil. Add the remaining 2 bay leaves, the onion, garlic, carrot, and celery; sauté gently until totally softened but not browned, about 10 minutes. Add the tomatoes and the ⅓ cup juices, salt, and pepper to taste. Bring to a boil and immediately reduce to a slow simmer. Cook gently until the sauce thickens, about 10 minutes.

Add the freshly cooked or canned beans and the 1 tablespoon liquid to the sauce. Bring to a boil again and immediately reduce to a simmer. Cover and cook gently to blend the flavors, an additional 10 to 15 minutes. Discard the bay leaves.

Transfer to a serving dish and sprinkle with the parsley. Serve hot or warm.

1-½ cups dried cannellini or Great
    Northern beans, or 3 cups drained,
    canned white beans plus 1 tablespoon
    of their liquid

4 large bay leaves

3 tablespoons extra-virgin olive oil

1 small onion, finely chopped

1 clove garlic, finely chopped

1 carrot, scraped and chopped

1 celery stalk, including the leaves, chopped

2-½ pounds vine-ripened plum tomatoes,
    peeled, seeded, and chopped, or
    1 can (28-ounces) plum tomatoes,
    seeded and chopped, plus ⅓ cup of
    their liquid

¾ teaspoon salt, or to taste

freshly milled black pepper

1 tablespoon chopped fresh Italian parsley

# FAGIOLI CON PECORINO AL FORNO

✷

### BAKED BABY LIMA BEANS WITH PECORINO

FOR 4 PEOPLE

Various types of beans can be used for this baked dish, including **CANNELLINI** or Great Northern beans. But I like the flavor of baby lima beans, which are easily found in American supermarkets. If they are difficult to find, large lima beans can be substituted.

2-½ cups (1 pound) dried baby
    lima beans

4 tablespoons unsalted butter

2 tablespoons extra-virgin olive oil

1 carrot, scraped and grated

1 yellow onion, chopped

2 green onions, including 3 inches of
    green tops, chopped

6 large fresh sage leaves, chopped, or
    ½ teaspoon crumbled dried sage

2 level tablespoons tomato paste

1-¾ teaspoons salt, or to taste

freshly milled white or black pepper

2 cups Vegetable Broth (page 58)

¼ pound semisoft pecorino such as
    Tuscan caciotta or fior di
    Sardegna, Spanish manchego, or
    other good, sharp semisoft cheese,
    finely shredded

½ cup fine dried bread crumbs, lightly
    toasted (page 17)

Rinse the beans, pick them over, and then rehydrate and cook them according to the directions on page 15. Be sure to simmer them gently; the beans have a tendency to disintegrate if not cooked delicately. Remove the beans from the heat when they are tender but still firm, and drain immediately. Do not rinse them, but set them aside to cool.

Preheat an oven to 400 degrees F. In a skillet over medium heat, melt the butter with the oil. Add the carrot, yellow onion, green onions, and sage. Sauté until the vegetables are softened, about 5 minutes. Stir in the tomato paste, salt, and pepper to taste. Add the drained beans and the broth. Cook gently for 15 minutes to marry the flavors.

Transfer the beans to an attractive baking dish large enough to accommodate them comfortably. In a small bowl stir together the cheese and the crumbs and sprinkle over the beans.

Bake until the cheese is melted and golden, 10 to 15 minutes. Serve immediately directly from the dish.

# CASSERUOLA DI LENTICCHIE

✦

## LENTIL CASSEROLE

### FOR 2 OR 3 PEOPLE

**T**HIS TASTY LENTIL DISH CAN BE A MAIN DISH FOR TWO OR THREE PEOPLE, OR A **CONTORNO** FOR FOUR. BY COOKING THE LENTILS AS YOU WOULD A **RISOTTO**, ADDING THE LIQUID A LITTLE AT A TIME RATHER THAN FIRST BOILING AND DRAINING THEM, ALL THE VITAMINS ARE RETAINED. THE DISH IS EXCELLENT MADE WITH BROTH, BUT IT IS ALSO SUCCESSFUL COOKED WITH WATER. THE GREEN ONIONS, GARLIC, CARROT, AND CELERY AND LEAVES CAN ALL BE CHOPPED TOGETHER ON A BIG CUTTING BOARD OR KITCHEN WORK SURFACE WITH A **MEZZALUNA** (HALF-MOON-SHAPED CHOPPER) OR A LARGE CHOPPING KNIFE. INCLUDING ABOUT THREE INCHES OF THE DARK GREEN PART OF THE GREEN ONION IMPARTS A GREAT DEAL OF FLAVOR TO THE FINISHED DISH.

In a flameproof earthenware casserole or a Dutch oven over medium heat, melt the butter with the olive oil. Add the green onions, garlic, carrot, parsley, and celery and leaves; sauté gently, stirring occasionally, until softened, about 12 minutes. Add the bay leaves, tomatoes, tomato paste, and 1 tablespoon of the broth to the skillet and stir to distribute the tomato paste.

Add the lentils to the vegetable mixture and stir over low heat. Add 1 cup of the broth and cover with the lid ajar. When the broth is absorbed, add another cup. Continue adding the broth in this manner until all of it has been absorbed, keeping the heat low all the while. Keep the pan partially covered when you are not adding liquid. The lentils should take about 40 minutes to cook from the time the first cup of broth is added.

Discard the bay leaves. Season with the pepper and salt. Transfer to a serving dish and serve hot.

*1 tablespoon unsalted butter*

*3 tablespoons extra-virgin olive oil*

*2 green onions, including 3 inches of green tops, finely chopped*

*1 clove garlic, scraped and finely chopped*

*1 small carrot, scraped and finely chopped*

*1 tablespoon finely chopped fresh Italian parsley*

*1 small celery stalk, including the leaves, finely chopped*

*2 bay leaves*

*½ cup peeled, seeded, and chopped fresh or canned plum tomatoes*

*1 tablespoon tomato paste*

*5 cups Vegetable Broth (page 58)*

*1-¼ cups (½ pound) lentils, rinsed and picked over*

*¼ teaspoon freshly milled black pepper*

*1 teaspoon salt*

# COTOLETTE DI FUNGHI

✺

## MUSHROOM "CUTLETS" STUFFED WITH FONTINA

FOR 3 PEOPLE

THESE CUTLETS" ARE SUBSTANTIAL ENOUGH TO BE A MAIN COURSE. IN ITALY, THE INCOMPARABLE **PORCINO** OR ANOTHER VARIETY OF WILD MUSHROOM CALLED **OVOLI** ARE USED. THESE ARE NOT EASY TO FIND IN AMERICA, BUT THIS MARVELOUS DISH CAN BE MADE WITH OTHER LARGE MUSHROOMS WITH FLAT CAPS, SUCH AS THE **PORTOBELLO**, A CULTIVATED MUSHROOM THAT IS NOW FAIRLY COMMON IN AMERICAN MARKETS. EVEN VERY LARGE CULTIVATED WHITE MUSHROOMS CAN BE USED.

*¾ pound large fresh mushrooms*

*¼ pound fontina, thinly sliced*

*2 eggs*

*½ teaspoon salt, plus salt to taste*

*freshly milled black pepper*

*1 cup fine dried bread crumbs, lightly*
*    toasted (page 17)*

*olive oil for frying*

Using a soft brush or clean kitchen towel, remove any dirt from the mushrooms. Do not wash them because water alters their texture. Remove their stems; use the stems for another purpose or, if you prefer, trim away any woody parts and cook the stems without the cheese along with the caps.

If the caps are large enough, slice them in half horizontally and place a *fontina* slice between the two halves. If you are using the smaller white mushroom variety, place a *fontina* slice between two caps. If necessary, use short pieces of toothpick to secure the mushroom "sandwich."

Break the eggs into a shallow bowl, add the salt and pepper, and beat with a fork to combine. Place the bread crumbs in a separate shallow bowl.

In a skillet over medium-high heat, pour in olive oil to a depth of ½ inch. Just before you are ready to begin frying, dip each "sandwich" into the beaten egg, then coat it thoroughly with the bread crumbs. When the oil is hot enough to make the mushrooms sizzle, slip the "sandwiches" into the oil. Do not crowd the pan. Fry, turning once, until crisp and golden on both sides, about 5 minutes on each side. Handle them gently, using a spatula and long fork to turn them. If you like, follow the same procedure with the stems. Remove to paper towels to drain briefly.

Remove any toothpicks, sprinkle with salt, and serve hot.

# CROSTATA DI CARCIOFI, PORRI, E FUNGHI

※

## ARTICHOKE, LEEK, AND MUSHROOM TART

FOR 4 TO 6 PEOPLE

**P**UFF PASTRY IS AN EXCEEDINGLY USEFUL THING TO HAVE ON HAND OR IN THE FREEZER FOR TARTS OF ALL KINDS, SAVORY AS WELL AS SWEET. THE NEAPOLITANS USE IT FOR MAKING SWEETS, BUT IN THE NORTH OF ITALY, CLOSE TO THE BORDERS OF FRANCE, ONE FINDS SAVORY TARTS SUCH AS THIS ONE. OTHER FILLINGS INCLUDE ONE OF **RICOTTA**, NUTMEG, COOKED CHOPPED SPINACH, AND **PARMIGIANO**, THE SAME CLASSIC COMBINATION THAT SO OFTEN APPEARS AS A STUFFING FOR RAVIOLI, **CANNELLONI**, AND OTHER TYPES OF FILLED PASTA. ※ CERTAINLY THE BEST PUFF PASTRY IS THAT WHICH IS MADE PROPERLY AT HOME. BUT IT TAKES TIME AND SKILL. VERY GOOD PUFF PASTRY IS OFTEN AVAILABLE AT BAKERIES OR IN THE FREEZER SECTION OF FOOD-SPECIALTY SHOPS. IF BUYING FROZEN PUFF PASTRY, CAREFULLY READ THE DIRECTIONS FOR THAWING BEFORE PROCEEDING WITH THIS RECIPE.

Have ready a large glass or ceramic bowl (do not use metal) filled with cold water to which you have added the lemon juice. Trim only a thin slice from the bottom of the stem of each artichoke to remove the dark skin. Pare off all the dark green skin on the stem. The flesh of the stem is good. With your hand, pull off the tough outer leaves until you reach leaves that have tender, white areas at their base. Cut off only the upper dark green part of the inner leaves; leave the light greenish yellow base. The inner rows of leaves are the tender part you want, so be careful not to cut away too much. Cut the artichoke in half lengthwise and, with a small knife, cut out the hairy choke and any other tough inner purple leaves. Immediately put the cleaned artichokes into the waiting acidulated water to prevent them from turning brown. When all of the artichokes have been trimmed, drain them. Place each artichoke half cut side down on a surface and cut lengthwise into slices ¼ inch thick.

Bring a large saucepan filled with water to a boil. Add the artichokes and 1 teaspoon salt and boil until tender but not mushy. Fresh, young artichokes will be ready in approximately 5 minutes; old, tough artichokes may take up to 10 to 12 minutes. Drain and allow to cool.

Preheat an oven to 400 degrees F. Line a baking sheet with parchment paper, or lightly oil the baking sheet.

*2 artichokes (about ½ pound each)*

*1 tablespoon freshly squeezed lemon juice or vinegar*

*salt*

*olive oil for oiling baking sheet (optional)*

*1 leek*

*¼ pound fresh cultivated mushrooms*

*3 tablespoons unsalted butter*

*2 tablespoons freshly grated parmigiano*

*2 tablespoons chopped fresh basil, or 1 tablespoon dried basil*

*¼ teaspoon salt, or to taste*

*freshly milled black pepper*

*about 1 pound puff pastry, chilled*

*3 ounces fontina, thinly sliced*

*1 egg, lightly beaten with 1 tablespoon milk*

Trim off the roots and the dark green tops from the leek and discard. Slice it in half lengthwise and spread open the sheaths under cold running water to wash any sand that is lodged between them. Slice thinly crosswise and set aside.

Using a soft brush or clean kitchen towel, remove any dirt from the mushrooms. Do not wash them because water will alter their texture. Trim off the tough bottoms from the stems and discard. Slice the mushrooms thinly. Set aside.

In a skillet over medium-low heat, melt 1 tablespoon of the butter. Add the leek and sauté until softened, 7 to 8 minutes. Using a slotted spoon, transfer the leek to a dish. Melt another tablespoon of butter in the skillet over medium-low heat. Add the cooked artichokes and sauté until colored, about 4 minutes. Using the slotted spoon, transfer them to the dish with the leeks.

Melt the remaining 1 tablespoon butter in the skillet and add the mushrooms. Sauté them gently until colored, 5 to 6 minutes. Using a slotted spoon, transfer them to the dish with the other vegetables. Add the *parmigiano*, basil, salt, and pepper to taste and allow the mixture to cool to room temperature.

Meanwhile, place the puff pastry on a lightly floured pastry board and roll it out lightly just to smooth out the creases. Cut it in half horizontally so that you have 2 squares or rectangles (the shape will depend upon the size of the premade pastry). Place the cooled filling in the middle of one of the pastry sheets, leaving a 1-inch border on all sides. Place the *fontina* slices over the filling. Brush the border with some of the egg-milk mixture. Place the second sheet of pastry on top and, using a fork, crimp the edges well all around to seal. Make several slashes on the top of the pastry and brush with some of the egg-milk mixture.

Transfer the tart to the prepared baking sheet. Bake until golden brown, 15 to 20 minutes. Transfer to a rack and allow to settle for 5 to 10 minutes before cutting into squares. Serve hot or warm.

# CROSTATA DI POMODORO

✾

FRESH TOMATO TART

MAKES TWO 10-INCH TARTS; SERVES 10 TO 12

HERE IS ANOTHER GOOD DISH TO MAKE IN THE SUMMER WHEN SWEET, VINE-RIPENED TOMATOES ARE AVAILABLE. THE TOPPING EVOKES A TOMATO PIZZA TOPPING, BUT THE DOUGH USED FOR THE **CROSTATA** PRODUCES A TRUE FLAKY TART CRUST.

To make the crust, in a mixing bowl, stir together the flour and salt. Using a pastry blender or 2 knives, cut in the butter until pea-shaped lumps form. Sprinkle the ice water over the top of the mixture, then work the water throughout the mixture by gently tossing with 2 forks. Using your hands, form 2 balls of dough. Be careful not to overhandle the dough.

To make the dough in a food processor, place the flour, salt, and butter in the food processor container fitted with the metal blade. Pulse until pea-sized pieces form. Pulse again while you add the water to the mixture. Stop when the dough pulls away from the walls of the processor and gather into a rough mass. Divide it in half and pat into 2 balls.

Put the dough balls in a loosely covered bowl or loosely covered plastic bag, leaving room for a little air to enter. Chill for 2 hours.

Preheat an oven to 375 degrees F. Lightly grease two 10-inch tart pans.

On a lightly floured board roll out 1 ball of dough into a disk large enough to cover the bottom and sides of the prepared pan; it will be about ⅛ inch thick. Drape the disk around the rolling pin and transfer it to the pan, pressing it gently onto the bottom and sides. (If desired, the pastry shell can be wrapped and frozen for up to 3 months.)

Line the pastry shell with half of the cheese slices, covering the bottom surface completely. Arrange some of the tomato slices in a circle over the cheese, overlapping them and beginning at the outer edge of the pan. Place a second circle of tomato slices inside the first circle, overlapping them in the same manner. Fill in the center area with another overlapping ring of tomato slices. Scatter some of the oregano and the olives, if using them, over the tomatoes. Sprinkle with the salt and pepper to taste, then drizzle with olive oil. Make

*For the crust:*

2-¼ cups unbleached all-purpose flour, chilled

1 teaspoon salt

14 tablespoons unsalted butter, chilled

6 tablespoons ice water


unsalted butter for greasing tart pans


*For the filling:*

1 pound mozzarella, thinly sliced

2 pounds ripe but firm vine-ripened tomatoes, thinly sliced

2 teaspoons chopped fresh oregano or thyme, or 1 teaspoon dried oregano or thyme

¼ cup sharply flavored imported black olives, pitted and sliced (optional)

½ teaspoon salt

freshly milled black pepper

extra-virgin olive oil for drizzling

a second tart in the same manner with the remaining ball of dough and filling ingredients.

Bake until the crust is golden, about 30 minutes. Remove from the oven and transfer to a rack to cool for about 10 minutes. Serve hot or warm, cut into wedges.

VARIATION: This tart can be made with other vegetables. Small eggplants are particularly suitable. Use 2 pounds eggplants and omit the olives. Leave the skins on the eggplants, but trim off and discard the stems and navels. Cut the eggplants crosswise into slices ¼ inch thick. Stand the slices upright in a colander, sprinkle with salt, and let drain for 40 minutes. Use a clean kitchen towel or paper towels to blot sweat and excess salt. Brush the slices with extra-virgin olive oil. Precook the slices for about 5 minutes in a preheated broiler or over a charcoal fire 6 to 8 inches from the heat source, turning once at the halfway point. Arrange the eggplant slices in a circular fashion as directed for the tomatoes. Proceed as directed with the recipe.

chapter five

CONTORNI E
INSALATE

side dishes and salads

CONTORNI MEANS, LITERALLY, "THAT WHICH SURROUNDS." Some *contorni* are almost inseparable from certain main courses because of a harmony of flavors that makes the two dishes especially satisfying when teamed. In my mother's kitchen, Sardinian as it was in flavor, this was the case with artichokes and lamb. Creamy potato purée, cooked with hot milk, butter, and grated *parmigiano* added just before serving, is often served with an *intingolo*, a savory sauce or concoction, while lentils cooked in a tomato sauce are lovely on a plate with sausages. Traditionally, the *contorno*—one or more—accompanies meat, poultry, game, or fish dishes. For the vegetarian, *contorni* might also function as *intermezzi*, that is, separate dishes served between other courses.

The limited offerings on tourist menus disguise how creative and extensive the repertoire of *contorni* is on the Italian table. This is perhaps because many vegetable dishes are treated as independent dishes, usually offered as *antipasti*, rather than side dishes. Stuffed vegetables, *fritto misto di verdura* (deep-fried vegetables), cooked vegetable salads, many mushroom dishes, and anything dressed with mayonnaise, for example, usually fall into the *antipasto* category. But the less complex vegetable and bean side dishes are most useful as accompaniments.

Southern Italy is particularly prolific when it comes to *contorni* because the cuisines of those poor regions are primarily vegetable-based. Certain vegetables, such as *cime di rape* (broccoli rape), are barely known in the north.

The tomato, while far from unknown in the north, is particularly prominent in the south. The hot, even torrid, dry climate of these regions produces the sweetest and most succulent tomatoes. It should not be assumed, however, that tomatoes and tomato sauce dishes are as prevalent in southern cooking as one would think from looking at the typical menu of American-Italian eateries. Tomatoes might appear as components of a vegetable stew that is served as a *contorno*, such as in My Mother's Stewed Pumpkin with Garlic and Black Olives (page 135), but tomato sauce does not ubiquitously cover stewed vegetables, as one would be wont to think based on the example of American-Italian cooking.

A universal criticism of Italian vegetable side dishes is that they are overcooked. It is true that the Italians cook vegetables longer than the Americans or the Chinese do, for example, and they are often dogmatic on this point. I once attended a cooking class held by a well-known Italian teacher. One of the students complained the vegetables were overcooked for her taste, which caused the *maestro* to blaspheme non-Italian practices to such a point that the young woman, who maintained her ground, never returned. I think there is a case for moderation here. I find myself cooking vegetables for less time than most Italians would. On the other hand, I do not think that vegetables are appealing when they are half-raw. In many cases, such undercooking doesn't allow vegetables to sweeten. This is certainly true of broccoli, asparagus, and green beans, for example. Do Americans, for example, cook corn only halfway? Corn is cooked just to the point where the starches turn to sugar, but not so much that the corn loses its "bite." I use this principle as a guide in all vegetable cookery.

A second point concerning the cooking of vegetables is that Italians usually boil rather than steam them. Boiling in salted water insures that vegetables retain their brilliant color. Some of the nutrients are lost in the cooking water, however. The steaming method, on the other hand, preserves the nutrients. Cooking vegetables in butter or oil or stewing them also keeps nutrients intact. I steam such vegetables as cauliflower, cabbage, or beets, but I boil green vegetables. Respecting these distinctions, most of the recipes in this book call for boiling vegetables in the traditional Italian way, but they can be steamed, if preferred.

As far as cooking methods go, there isn't a single one that isn't employed with vegetables in the Italian kitchen. Virtually all vegetables are boiled, steamed, sautéed, fried and batter-fried, roasted, broiled, grilled, and baked. A classic treatment is to parboil vegetables first, then drain and sauté them in butter or olive oil. When sautéing in olive oil, garlic is often added to the pan. Another standard treatment is to parboil the vegetables and then bake them in a generously buttered baking dish with more butter and some freshly grated *parmigiano* on top. This method is particularly popular with Belgian endive, fennel, and asparagus.

✹

While the first course of an Italian meal, the *antipasto*, is designed to stimulate the palate, the last course, the salad, is meant to relax and refresh it. Thus it is served after the *secondo*, and sometimes with the *secondo* as a raw *contorno*.

Italian leafy salads generally contain no nuts, croutons, cheese, bacon, or other such additions. *Insalata verde* is a simple salad of one type of green. A more elaborate green salad, called *insalata mista*, usually contains more than one variety of lettuce or other greens, including sweet and bitter leaves, for contrast, and shredded carrot, sliced underripe tomatoes, thinly sliced *finocchio* (fennel) and/or celery, and a little thinly sliced sweet onion.

Salad dressing in Italy consists of nothing more than the best extra-virgin olive oil available, only a touch of vinegar, and salt (no pepper). Rather than mix the oil and vinegar together, the oil is distributed through the greens first, to coat the leaves and thus prevent them from wilting quickly. Then a little vinegar and salt are tossed in.

A relatively modern innovation is to add *gorgonzola* cheese to the dressing for a simple green salad. To do this, place a small amount of either young or ripe *gorgonzola* in the olive oil for the salad. Use a fork to mash the cheese into the oil. Coat the lettuce with this combination, then add a touch of wine vinegar and salt. Additional *gorgonzola* can be crumbled and tossed in after this. The cheese and the greens are very compatible. Combining them is like serving two courses in one, the salad course and cheese, which usually follow each another before the fruit is served.

Other types of raw salads, such as shredded carrots with lemon and olive oil, mushroom salad, tomato salad, and so on, might be served as *antipasti* or as salads. Vegetable salads that are charged with flavor, such as the Piedmontese Salad of Roasted Peppers, Olives, and *Fontina*, in chapter 2, are offered in the beginning of the meal where they serve to stimulate the appetite rather than soothe it.

Cauliflower and broccoli are never eaten raw, as they are in America. If they are made into salads, they are first cooked, then dressed with olive oil and lemon juice rather than vinegar.

Cooked vegetable salads might be served as *antipasti* or as a salad course after the *secondo*. Asparagus and green beans, in particular, are typically boiled and dressed with fruity olive oil and lemon as a salad course.

# ORZO AL BECCO

❀

BARLEY "RICE"

FOR 4 OR 5 PEOPLE

THIS IS A FACSIMILE OF A SIDE DISH I ATE WITH **OSSO BUCO,** THE CLASSIC VEAL SHANK DISH OF MILAN, IN THE DELIGHTFUL BECCO, A MANHATTAN ITALIAN RESTAURANT RUN BY LIDIA BASTIANICH AND HER SON, JOSEPH. **OSSO BUCO** IS USUALLY SERVED WITH **RISOTTO ALLA MILANESE,** A SPLENDID **RISOTTO** FLAVORED WITH BEEF MARROW, WINE, AND SAFFRON. BUT THE BARLEY THE BASTIANICHES SERVED WITH **OSSO BUCO** WAS IMMENSELY FLAVORFUL AND BEAUTIFUL TO LOOK AT, SPECKED WITH CHOPPED VEGETABLES IN WHICH IT HAD BEEN SAUTÉED. NOT OVERCOOKING THE VEGETABLES IS ESSENTIAL TO THE SUCCESS OF THIS DISH, AND SO IS USING AUTHENTIC **PARMIGIANO-REGGIANO.**

*1 cup medium pearl barley (see note)*

*3 cups water*

*1 tablespoon, plus 2 teaspoons salt*

*2 large or 3 medium bay leaves*

*1 large carrot, scraped and cut into very small dice*

*2 celery stalks, including leaves, cut into very small dice*

*½ red bell pepper, seeded, deribbed, and cut into very small dice*

*6-inch length zucchini, cored to remove seeds, peeled, and cut into very small dice*

*5 tablespoons unsalted butter*

*4 large shallots, cut into very small dice*

*⅓ cup Vegetable Broth (page 58)*

*freshly milled white pepper*

*⅓ cup freshly grated parmigiano*

Place the barley in a large strainer or colander and wash it in cold running water. Transfer it to a pot with the 3 cups water, the 1 tablespoon salt, and the bay leaves. Bring to a boil, then reduce to a simmer. Cook uncovered over medium-low heat until the barley is just about cooked but not mushy, 40 to 45 minutes. Drain and rinse well with cold water; this is necessary in order to remove excess starch that would affect the texture of the dish. Set aside.

Meanwhile, bring a saucepan full of water to a boil and add the 2 teaspoons salt. Drop in all the diced vegetables, except for the shallots, and cook for 1 to 2 minutes; drain immediately and set aside.

In a large skillet over medium-low heat, melt 3 tablespoons of the butter. Add the shallots and sauté gently until softened, 6 to 8 minutes. Add the blanched vegetables and stir to combine them with the shallots. Add the barley and continue to sauté over medium-low heat for 4 to 5 minutes. Add the broth and cook over low heat, stirring frequently, until it is absorbed, about 4 minutes. Taste for salt and add pepper to taste.

Remove the skillet from the heat and gently stir in the remaining 2 tablespoons butter and the cheese. Remove and discard the bay leaves, transfer to a serving dish, and serve immediately.

NOTE: Medium pearl barley, commonly found in American markets, has been processed to reduce its cooking time. This process strips away some of its nutrients. Whole barley, found in health-food stores, takes twice as long to cook.

# PEPERONI ARROSTITI

❀

## MARINATED ROASTED BELL PEPPERS

### FOR 6 TO 8 PEOPLE

THE FLAVORS OF BELL PEPPERS INTENSIFY TREMENDOUSLY WHEN THE PEPPERS ARE ROASTED, WHICH MAKES THEM IDEAL FOR **ANTIPASTI**. BUT DON'T BE AFRAID TO SERVE THEM AS A SIDE DISH. BECAUSE THE PEPPERS ARE SO SWEET, THEY ARE AGREEABLE COMPANIONS TO MANY VEGETARIAN MAIN COURSES. FOR EXAMPLE, THEY ARE PARTICULARLY HAPPY WITH **FRITTATE** AND OTHER EGG DISHES, AND MAKE A LOVELY CONTRAST TO THE NUTTY FLAVOR OF **POLENTA** (NOT TO MENTION THE STUNNING COLOR COMBINATION OF THE REDS OF THE PEPPERS WITH THE YELLOW OF EGG DISHES OR **POLENTA**). ROASTED PEPPERS ARE EASILY MADE IN ADVANCE AND KEPT, REFRIGERATED, FOR SEVERAL DAYS. I SUGGEST RED, YELLOW, OR ORANGE BELL PEPPERS BECAUSE THEY ARE SWEETER THAN THE GREEN ONES.

Roast the bell peppers and peel, stem, seed, and derib as directed on page 33. Cut the peppers into strips 2 inches long by ¼ inch wide. Place them in a shallow bowl and add the oil, garlic, and parsley, tossing gently to coat evenly. Allow the peppers to marinate for several hours at room temperature, or overnight. Serve at room temperature.

VERSIONE CON SEDANO (VARIATION WITH CELERY HEARTS): This variation may be served as a *contorno*, as a salad, or as an *antipasto*. Trim off the tough base from 6 celery hearts. Cut the hearts on the diagonal into very thin slices. Toss with the roasted peppers, oil, garlic, and parsley. Add ¼ cup sharply flavored imported black olives, pitted and sliced, if desired. Serve immediately.

*8 large red, yellow, or orange bell peppers, or a mixture*
*3 tablespoons extra-virgin olive oil*
*4 large cloves garlic, bruised*
*1 tablespoon chopped fresh Italian parsley*

# VERDURA AL FORNO

✤

## ROASTED VEGETABLES

FOR 6 TO 8 PEOPLE

VIRTUALLY ALL VEGETABLES CAN BE ROASTED, AND WHILE MANY FASHIONABLE RESTAURANTS HAVE CAUGHT ON TO THE VIRTUES OF PREPARING VEGETABLES THIS WAY, THE METHOD IS UNFA-MILIAR TO MOST HOME COOKS. IT IS AN EXCELLENT MEANS FOR COOKING VEGETABLES BECAUSE THE HIGH, DRY HEAT INTENSIFIES THE NATURAL FLAVORS (SEE NOTE). USE ANY OR ALL OF THE FOLLOWING VEGETABLES, OR TRY OTHERS OF YOUR OWN CHOOSING. IT IS IMPORTANT THAT ANY VEGETABLE YOU SELECT BE VERY FRESH, INCLUDING THE GARLIC; DON'T USE HEADS OF GARLIC THAT HAVE BEEN SIT-TING IN THE PANTRY FOR MONTHS. THE VEGETABLES CAN BE SERVED AS SIDE DISHES, ON A PLATTER AS AN **ANTIPASTO** COURSE, OR ALL TOGETHER ON A PLATTER FOR A VEGETARIAN MAIN COURSE. THE ROASTED GARLIC SHOULD BE SQUEEZED OUT OF THE CLOVES AND SPREAD DIRECTLY ONTO FRESH BREAD OR ONTO **CROSTINI**, THEN DRIZZLED WITH EXTRA-VIRGIN OLIVE OIL AND SPRINKLED WITH SALT. ✤ROASTED VEGETABLES ARE PERFECTLY DELICIOUS EATEN WITHOUT ANY CONDIMENT, ALTHOUGH OLIVE OIL, SALT, PEPPER, AND LEMON JUICE OR PARSLEY ARE SOMETIMES SPRINKLED ON THEM. OR, IF YOU LIKE, YOU CAN SMEAR THEM WITH A LITTLE **PESTO** (PAGE 75), LIKE THE GENOESE DO, BUT BE SPARING!

---

*1 pound asparagus*

*1 head radicchio*

*4 heads Belgian endive*

*4 small tomatoes*

*2 small zucchini*

*2 small eggplants*

*2 bulbs fennel, stalks and fronds*
*removed*

*2 whole heads garlic*

*2 medium-sized or large leeks*

*extra-virgin olive oil for brushing on*
*vegetables, basting, and drizzling*

*sea salt*

*freshly milled black pepper*

Preheat an oven to 450 degrees F.

Peel and trim the asparagus as directed on page 34. Trim off the base from the *radicchio* but leave the core intact. Cut the head lengthwise into 4 wedges. Likewise, trim off the base of the endives and slice them in half lengthwise. Trim and cut round or oval vegetables—tomatoes, eggplants, zucchini, fennel bulbs—in half or in quarters lengthwise, depending upon their size (baby zuc-chini can be roasted whole).

Remove excess paper from the whole garlic heads. Using a sharp knife, slice off about ½ inch from the top of each garlic head to expose most of cloves. Place the garlic heads in a small pan with water to cover. Bring to a boil, then reduce the heat to low and simmer gently, uncovered, for 10 minutes. Drain well, then brush whole garlic heads with olive oil and wrap tightly in aluminum foil.

Trim off the roots and the dark green tops of the leeks and discard them. Slice them in half lengthwise and spread open the sheaths under cold running water to wash out any sand that is lodged between them.

Brush the vegetables generously with olive oil on both sides. Place the vegetables on 2 or 3 baking sheets, being sure that there is plenty of room around each piece so that they will color nicely instead of steaming. Place the baking sheets on the middle rack of the oven. Baking time will depend upon the vegetables. They are cooked when they are tender but firm, in approximately these times: tomatoes in 15 to 20 minutes; asparagus in 20 to 30 minutes, depending upon their thickness; *radicchio*, Belgian endives, and zucchini in 30 to 35 minutes; eggplant in 30 to 35 minutes; leeks and fennel in 40 to 45 minutes.

Remove the cooked vegetables from the oven. Unwrap the garlic heads and arrange them and all the remaining vegetables in an attractive way on a platter. Except for the whole garlic heads, drizzle the vegetables with additional extra-virgin olive oil and sprinkle to taste with salt and pepper. If desired, sprinkle with parsley. Serve hot, warm, or at room temperature.

NOTE: Grilling is also a common—and ancient—method of cooking vegetables in Italy and other parts of the Mediterranean. This subject was covered in detail in my book *Antipasti: The Little Dishes of Italy.*

*chopped fresh Italian parsley for sprinkling on vegetables (optional)*

# CAROTE AL LATTE

✦

CARROTS COOKED IN MILK

FOR 4 PEOPLE

COOKING CARROTS IN MILK ADDS SWEETNESS AND BODY.  MY MOTHER OFTEN PREPARES CARROTS THIS WAY, ADDING FRESH MINT OR PARSLEY AT THE END.  I LIKE THIS DISH WITH TARRAGON, TOO, BECAUSE ITS SLIGHTLY ANISEY FLAVOR BRINGS OUT THE NATURAL SWEETNESS OF THE CARROTS.  USE FRESH TARRAGON IF IT IS AVAILABLE; OTHERWISE, SUBSTITUTE DRIED TARRAGON.  TARRAGON IS ONE OF THE FEW HERBS THAT DRIES SUCCESSFULLY.  ITS SWEETNESS DOESN'T DIE, AND ITS ORGINAL FLAVOR IS STILL INTACT.

*1 pound young carrots, tops removed and*
*scraped*
*½ teaspoon salt*
*2 tablespoons unsalted butter*
*¼ cup milk*
*½ teaspoon chopped fresh mint, Italian*
*parsley, or tarragon, or ¼ teaspoon*
*dried tarragon*
*freshly milled white or black pepper*

Cut the carrots into thin sticks 2 to 2-½ inches long.  Bring a saucepan three-fourths full of water to a rolling boil.  Drop in the carrots and the salt and bring to a boil again.  Cover partially and cook for another 10 minutes or so.  They should be cooked but still somewhat resistant to the bite.  Drain well.

Return the carrots to the saucepan and add the butter, milk, and herb.  Place over medium-low heat just long enough for the butter to melt and the milk to be absorbed.  Taste for salt.  Add pepper to taste.  Remove to a serving dish and serve immediately.

# FUNGHI TRIFOLATI

✸

SAUTÉED MUSHROOMS

FOR 6 PEOPLE

THIS WAY OF COOKING MUSHROOMS IS AN INDELIBLE PART OF MY CHILDHOOD MEMORIES OF SUNDAY DINNER, WHICH WAS USUALLY A ROAST OF SOME KIND OR OTHER—LAMB, PORK, BEEF, VEAL, OR CHICKEN. THE MUSHROOMS WERE SERVED FIRST AS AN **ANTIPASTO**, OR IF ANOTHER **ANTIPASTO** WAS SUBSTITUTED, THEY WOULD BE BROUGHT TO THE TABLE ALONG WITH THE ROAST. NEARLY EVERY DINNER GUEST FOR WHOM I COOK THESE MUSHROOMS IS SURPRISED AND DELIGHTED BY THIS TREATMENT, SO I OFFER IT HERE. IN ITALY, PRIZED WILD **PORCINI** WOULD BE USED, BUT THEY ARE NEARLY IMPOSSIBLE TO FIND IN AMERICA. SUBSTITUTE WILD MUSHROOMS IF YOU CAN, TO MAKE THE TEXTURES AND FLAVORS INTERESTING; OR, IF NECESSARY, COMBINE WILD MUSHROOMS WITH CULTIVATED MUSHROOMS. ✸ IN LIGURIA, THESE MUSHROOMS, SAUTÉED IN BUTTER RATHER THAN OLIVE OIL WITH THE ADDITION OF A LITTLE MARJORAM OR OREGANO, ARE SOMETIMES SERVED ON BUTTERED TOASTS—**CROSTINI**—AND OFFERED AS AN **ANTIPASTO**. THE DISH IS CALLED **FUNGHI AL FUNGHETTO**. ✸ I INCLUDE TWO METHODS FOR SAUTÉING MUSHROOMS. THE FIRST IS APPROPRIATE FOR BOTH WILD AND CULTIVATED MUSHROOMS. THE SECOND IS BEST FOR WILD MUSHROOMS THAT HAVE LONGER COOKING REQUIREMENTS. **CHANTERELLES**, OYSTER MUSHROOMS, MORELS, AND, OF COURSE, FRESH **PORCINI**, IF YOU CAN GET THEM, ARE MOST SUITABLE FOR THIS DISH. **SHIITAKES** WILL DO IF MIXED WITH ANY OF THESE OTHER VARIETIES, BUT ALONE THEY ARE SOMEWHAT BLAND AND NOT ENOUGH OF A COUNTERPOINT TO THE OREGANO, SAGE, AND THYME.

METHOD 1 Using a soft brush or a clean kitchen towel, remove any dirt from the mushrooms. Do not wash them because water alters their texture. Remove and discard any tough stems or woody parts. Slice the mushrooms thinly.

Place the garlic, parsley, and olive oil in a cold skillet, preferably nonstick, large enough to accommodate all the mushrooms later without overcrowding. Turn on the heat to low and sauté the garlic until softened but not colored, about 4 minutes. Add the mushrooms and, using a wooden spoon, toss to coat with the oil mixture on all sides. Sauté the mushrooms in this manner until they are softened and release their liquid into the pan, 8 to 10 minutes. Raise the heat to medium and continue cooking until the mushroom liquid evaporates, 2 or 3 minutes. Add salt and pepper to taste. Serve hot.

*1 pound fresh mushrooms (see recipe introduction)*

*3 large cloves garlic, finely chopped*

*3 tablespoons finely chopped fresh Italian parsley*

*3 tablespoons extra-virgin olive oil*

*salt*

*freshly milled black pepper*

VARIATION: For a Roman dish, add ½ cup pine nuts to the skillet 2 or 3 minutes before the mushrooms are done.

METHOD 2   Using a soft brush or a clean kitchen towel, remove any dirt from the mushrooms. Do not wash them because water alters their texture. Remove and discard any tough stems or woody parts. Slice the mushrooms thinly.

Place the oil and garlic in a cold skillet, preferably nonstick, large enough to accommodate all the mushrooms later without overcrowding. Turn on the heat to low and sauté the garlic gently until softened but not colored, about 4 minutes. Add the mushrooms, herbs, salt, and pepper to taste; using a wooden spoon, toss to coat with the oil mixture on all sides. Add the ¼ cup water, cover, and cook gently until tender, 15 to 30 minutes, depending upon the variety and freshness of the mushrooms. If the mushrooms seem to be drying out, add more water. No more than an additional 3 to 4 tablespoons should be necessary.

Taste for seasonings. Serve hot.

1 pound fresh wild mushrooms (see recipe introduction)

3 tablespoons extra-virgin olive oil

2 large cloves garlic, finely chopped or passed through a garlic press

1 teaspoon chopped fresh oregano, or ½ teaspoon dried oregano

1 teaspoon chopped fresh sage or thyme, or ½ teaspoon dried sage or thyme

¼ teaspoon salt

freshly milled black pepper

¼ cup water, or as needed

# ZUCCA CON OLIVE

✤

## MY MOTHER'S STEWED PUMPKIN WITH GARLIC AND BLACK OLIVES

FOR 6 PEOPLE

THE COMBINATION OF PUMPKIN, OLIVES, AND TOMATOES MAY SOUND UNUSUAL TO AMERICANS, BUT IT IS A SUPERB COMBINATION IN THIS GARLICKY **CONTORNO**. USE EATING-VARIETY SUGAR PUMPKINS (NOT THE STANDARD HALLOWEEN PUMPKINS, WHICH ARE STRINGY AND THIN) OR A HUBBARD SQUASH. THE FLAVOR OF THE PUMPKIN OR SQUASH ALONE IS BLAND, BUT YOU CAN GIVE IT GREAT CHARACTER BY MIXING IT WITH OLIVES, OLIVE OIL, GARLIC, AND TOMATO. IT IS BEST TO MAKE THIS DISH A DAY OR TWO BEFORE YOU PLAN TO SERVE IT AND KEEP IT IN THE REFRIGERATOR. THAT WAY, THE FLAVORS HAVE TIME TO MELD AND THE DISH WILL TASTE BETTER. SERVE ALONGSIDE A MAIN COURSE THAT DOES NOT CONTAIN TOMATO SAUCE.

In a saucepan over medium-low heat, warm the oil and garlic together until the garlic is fragrant, about 1 minute. Add the tomato sauce, stir, and bring slowly to a simmer, about 4 minutes. Add the squash, olives, thyme, and water. Cover partially and simmer gently until tender, about 30 minutes.

Season with the salt and pepper to taste. Serve immediately.

AHEAD-OF-TIME NOTE: This dish may be made up to 3 days in advance, cooled, covered, and refrigerated. Reheat over low heat.

¼ cup extra-virgin olive oil

3 large cloves garlic, chopped

1 cup canned tomato sauce, or ½ cup tomato paste mixed with ½ cup water

1 medium-sized butternut or Hubbard squash or 1 small pumpkin (about 1-½ pounds), peeled, seeded, and cut into 1-inch dice

12 oil-cured sharply flavored black olives (wrinkled variety if possible), pitted and halved

½ teaspoon chopped fresh thyme, or ¼ teaspoon dried thyme

¾ cup water

½ teaspoon salt

freshly milled black pepper

# ZUCCHINE GIALLE
# IN PADELLA

✵

YELLOW SUMMER SQUASH WITH HERBS

FOR 4 PEOPLE

**I**T IS IMPORTANT THAT THE SQUASHES BE FRESH, FIRM, AND YOUNG.  LARGE, SEEDY SUMMER SQUASHES WILL SIMPLY NOT DO.

*1-½ pounds (about 4) small yellow*
*summer squashes*
*2 to 3 tablespoons unsalted butter*
*1 onion, quartered and thinly sliced*
*½ teaspoon salt, or to taste*
*3 tablespoons water*
*1 tablespoon chopped fresh mint, basil,*
*or tarragon, or 1-½ teaspoons dried*
*tarragon*
*freshly milled white or black pepper*

Wash the squashes well to remove any imbedded dirt.  Cut them in half lengthwise.  If they have large or an excessive amount of seeds, remove them.  Thinly slice the squashes crosswise, or dice into ½-inch pieces.  Set aside.

In a skillet over medium heat, melt the butter.  Add the onion and sauté until it wilts, about 5 minutes.  Add the squashes and salt and toss together with the onion over high heat.

Reduce the heat to medium-low and add the water.  Stir and cover tightly.  Cook until tender, 15 minutes if the squash is very young and fresh, or 20 minutes if it is old or was large when it was picked.  Remove the cover once or twice during the cooking to stir the contents.

Mix in the herb and add pepper to taste.  Adjust with salt.  Serve immediately.

# CARCIOFI STUFATI CON PREZZEMOLO, AGLIO, E PISELLI

✳

MY MOTHER'S STEWED ARTICHOKES WITH PARSLEY, GARLIC, AND PEAS

FOR 3 OR 4 PEOPLE

ITALIAN ARTICHOKES ARE SMALL AND TENDER, AND HAVE NO CHOKE. UNFORTUNATELY, ARTICHOKES HERE ARE GROWN FOR SIZE, NOT QUALITY. BY THE TIME WE GET THEM, THEY ARE OFTEN ALMOST TOO TOUGH TO BOTHER WITH. BUY THE FRESHEST, BRIGHTEST GREEN ARTICHOKES AVAILABLE. AVOID THOSE THAT ARE EXCESSIVELY BROWN OR AT ALL WRINKLED, FOR THEY WILL BE TOUGH.

Prepare the artichokes as directed on page 119 up to the point where they are fully cleaned and in acidulated water. Drain the artichokes and cut each artichoke half lengthwise into 4 equal wedges. Pat dry.

In a large saucepan over medium heat, warm the olive oil. Add the garlic and sauté until softened, about 4 minutes. Add the artichokes, parsley, and thyme and stir with a wooden spoon. Pour in the ½ cup water and bring to a boil. Add the salt and pepper to taste. Reduce to a simmer, cover, and cook until tender, 10 to 15 minutes; the length of time will depend upon the freshness of the artichokes. If the artichokes seem to be drying out, add more water. If you think there is too much liquid once the chokes are half-cooked, remove the cover and cook over medium heat until some of it evaporates. Be sure to stir to prevent sticking. Add the peas 5 minutes before the artichokes are finished cooking.

Taste and adjust with salt and pepper. Serve immediately.

*3 large artichokes (about ½ pound each)*

*1 tablespoon extra-virgin olive oil*

*1 large clove garlic, finely chopped*

*1 tablespoon chopped fresh Italian parsley*

*½ teaspoon chopped fresh thyme, or*
*¼ teaspoon dried thyme*

*½ to ¾ cup water*

*½ teaspoon salt*

*freshly milled white or black pepper*

*1 cup fresh or frozen shelled peas*

# FAGIOLINI CON PINOLI

✳

## GREEN BEANS WITH PINE NUTS

FOR 6 PEOPLE

I USE **PINOLI** (PINE NUTS) LIBERALLY IN VEGETABLE COOKING; THE CREAMY RICHNESS OF THE TOASTED NUTS IS A NICE CONTRAST TO THE FLAVORS AND TEXTURES OF MANY VEGETABLES. I ESPECIALLY LIKE THE COMBINATION OF **PINOLI** AND GREEN BEANS, WHICH CAN BE SERVED EITHER HOT OR AT ROOM TEMPERATURE. TO SERVE AT ROOM TEMPERATURE, SUBSTITUTE EXTRA-VIRGIN OLIVE OIL FOR THE BUTTER AND SERVE THE DISH AS A SALAD.

*2 pounds young green beans, ends
    trimmed*

*1 tablespoon salt*

*2 tablespoons unsalted butter*

*1 tablespoon extra-virgin olive oil*

*⅓ cup pinoli (pine nuts), lightly
    toasted*

In a saucepan, bring enough water to cover the beans to a rolling boil. Add the beans and salt. Cook until tender, 6 to 7 minutes, then drain well.

In a skillet over medium heat, melt the butter with the oil. Add the beans and nuts to the pan and toss together. Serve at once.

# FAGIOLINI AL LIMONE

✱

GREEN BEANS WITH EGG AND LEMON SAUCE

FOR 4 PEOPLE

THIS IS ONE OF MY MOTHER'S WAYS OF COOKING GREEN BEANS. THE EGG AND LEMON PRODUCE A TANGY, SILKY SAUCE THAT HAS A REAL AFFINITY WITH THE TASTE AND TEXTURE OF GOOD FRESH GREEN BEANS.

½ pound young green beans, ends
   trimmed

2 teaspoons salt, plus salt to taste

1 tablespoon unsalted butter

2 small eggs

¼ cup freshly squeezed lemon juice

grated zest of ½ small lemon

freshly milled black pepper

salt

In a saucepan bring enough water to cover the beans generously to a rolling boil. Add the beans and the 2 teaspoons salt. Cook until tender, 6 to 7 minutes, then drain well.

In a saucepan over medium heat, melt the butter. Add the drained beans to the butter, toss to coat, and cover the pan to keep them hot. In a bowl lightly beat the eggs, and then beat in the lemon juice, lemon zest, and pepper to taste. Add the egg mixture to the hot beans and stir quickly with a wooden spoon. To prevent the eggs from curdling, keep the pot over the lowest possible heat, or place a flame tamer over the burner. As soon as the sauce thickens, remove the pot from the flame.

Add salt. Serve hot.

VERSIONE CON ASPARAGI (VARIATION WITH ASPARAGUS): Trim and cook the asparagus as directed on page 34. Substitute the asparagus for the beans in the recipe. Take care when stirring the asparagus with the sauce not to bruise or break the delicate tips.

# FRITTELLE DI CAVOLFIORE

❀

CAULIFLOWER FRITTERS

FOR 4 TO 5 PEOPLE

PROPERLY DEEP FRIED VEGETABLES ARE ONE OF THE MOST IRRESISTIBLE OF FOODS AND THE ITAL-IANS ARE PARTICULARLY ADEPT AT PREPARING THEM. THERE ARE MANY DIFFERENT METHODS FOR DEEP-FRYING, AND MANY TYPES OF VEGETABLES ARE USED. I OFFER TWO METHODS HERE, BOTH USING CAULIFLOWER. IN THE FIRST, THE CAULIFLOWER IS DIPPED IN FLOUR, THEN DIPPED IN EGG, AND THEN IN FLOUR AGAIN, AND DEEP-FRIED IN OLIVE OIL. IN THE SECOND METHOD, BREAD CRUMBS REPLACE FLOUR FOR THE SECOND COATING. MUSHROOMS (SMALL WHOLE ONES OR THICKLY SLICED LARGER ONES), FENNEL, AND ARTICHOKES (DIRECTIONS FOLLOW) ARE PARTICULARLY DELECTABLE FRIED WITH THIS SECOND COATING. MANY OTHER VEGETABLES ARE FRIED IN THIS MANNER. SOME, LIKE CELERY, MUST BE PARBOILED FIRST; OTHERS, SUCH AS ZUCCHINI AND EGGPLANT, NEED NO PRECOOKING. THE SECOND METHOD PRODUCES A CRUNCHIER COATING, WHILE THE FIRST IS A LITTLE MORE DELICATE. ❀ BE SURE THE VEGETABLES ARE DRIED THOROUGHLY BEFORE COATING AND FRYING; VEGETABLES THAT ARE PARTIALLY COOKED BEFORE FRYING SHOULD BE THOROUGHLY DRAINED AND PATTED DRY BEFORE COAT-ING AND FRYING. ❀ BATTER-FRYING, ANOTHER DELECTABLE WAY OF COOKING VEGETABLES, IS DESCRIBED ON PAGE 50.

METHOD 1  In a large saucepan, bring the water to a rolling boil. Meanwhile, remove and discard the core and leaves from the cauliflower. Divide the cauli-flower into florets. Add the 1 tablespoon salt and the cauliflower to the boiling water. Cover and boil until half-cooked, about 6 minutes. Drain well, allow to cool, and pat dry.

In a large skillet, pour in olive oil to a depth of 1-½ inches and place over medium-high heat. In a shallow bowl, or on waxed paper on the kitchen counter, place the flour and mix in pepper to taste. Break the eggs into a bowl and beat lightly with a fork. When the oil is hot enough to make the cauliflower sizzle, dredge each floret in the flour, dip it into the eggs, then dip it in the flour again, shaking off any excess. Slip the florets into the hot oil, being careful not to crowd the pan. Fry on both sides, turning once, until golden, about 4 minutes on each side. Using a slotted spoon, remove to paper towels to drain briefly.

Sprinkle with salt to taste and serve immediately.

*4 quarts water*

*1 small head cauliflower (about 1 pound)*

*1 tablespoon salt, plus salt to taste*

*olive oil for deep-frying*

*¾ cup all-purpose flour*

*freshly milled black or white pepper*

*2 extra-large eggs*

1 small head cauliflower (about 1
    pound)
1 tablespoon salt, plus salt to taste
olive oil for deep-frying
½ cup all-purpose flour
freshly milled black or white pepper
2 extra-large eggs
1 cup fine dried white bread crumbs,
    lightly toasted (page 17)

METHOD 2 Follow Method 1 up through parboiling and draining the cauli-flower. Heat the oil and ready the flour and eggs as directed. Place the bread crumbs in a shallow bowl. Dredge each floret in the seasoned flour, then dip in the beaten egg. Now roll the florets in the bread crumbs instead of the flour. Fry, drain on paper towels, and serve as directed.

FRITTELLE DI FINOCCHIO (FENNEL FRITTERS): Cut off the stalks and fronds from 2 bulbs fennel and reserve for another use. Trim off any brown spots. Slice a piece off the tough base of each bulb, being careful not to cut off too much of the base section that keeps the lower stalks intact. Cut the bulb length-wise into slices approximately ½ inch thick. Drop into boiling water to which 1 teaspoon salt has been added and boil until half-cooked, about 6 minutes. Drain well, allow to cool, and pat dry. Coat and fry as directed in Method 2.

FRITTELLE DI CARCIOFI (ARTICHOKE FRITTERS): Prepare 4 arti-chokes as directed on page 119 up to the point where they are fully cleaned and in acidulated water. Drain the artichokes and cut each half lengthwise into slices about ¼ inch thick. Drop into boiling water to which 1 teaspoon salt has been added and until half-cooked, about 5 minutes. Small, tender artichokes need parboiling for only 2 to 3 minutes. Drain well, allow to cool, and pat dry. Coat and fry as directed in Method 2.

# BROCCOLI ALL'OLIO E LIMONE

✽

## BROCCOLI WITH LEMON AND OLIVE OIL

### FOR 4 TO 6 PEOPLE

**D**RESSING COOKED VEGETABLES WITH FRUITY OLIVE OIL AND LEMON IS THE MOST UBIQUITOUS PREPARATION OF **CONTORNI**. I HESITATED AT FIRST TO INCLUDE SUCH AN OBVIOUS TREATMENT. BUT THINKING HOW OFTEN STUDENTS OR GUESTS AT MY HOME DELIGHT AT THE TASTE OF THIS SIMPLE WAY OF PREPARING BROCCOLI AND MANY OTHER VEGETABLES, I THOUGHT IT MUST BE PRESENTED HERE. AS WITH EVERY ITALIAN DISH, THE FRESHEST OF INGREDIENTS ARE ESSENTIAL, AND THE OLIVE OIL MUST BE VERY FRUITY. BUT A FEW OTHER THINGS ARE IMPORTANT TO REMEMBER: COOKING THE BROC-COLI IN SALTED WATER HELPS TO MAINTAIN ITS VIBRANT GREEN. ALSO, DRESSING THE VEGETABLES WITH THE OIL WHILE THEY ARE STILL WARM RELEASES THE OIL'S FRUITY FLAVOR.

Wash and trim the broccoli, cutting each head into separate but not-too-small florets. In a large saucepan bring plenty of water to a rolling boil. Add the salt and the broccoli and boil until tender, 7 to 9 minutes. Drain well immediately; excess water will dilute the precious virgin oil.

Transfer the broccoli to a serving dish and, while still hot, dress with the olive oil to taste (just as you would a salad). Serve lemon wedges on the side; don't sprinkle the broccoli with lemon beforehand, or it will turn brown. Sprinkle with pepper to taste. Let each person squeeze lemon onto his or her own portion. Serve warm or at room temperature.

*1 head broccoli (about 1-¼ pounds)*
*1 tablespoon salt*
*extra-virgin olive oil*
*2 lemons, cut into wedges*
*freshly milled black pepper*

# CIME DI RAPE IN PADELLA

✿

SAUTÉED BROCCOLI RAPE

FOR 6 PEOPLE

**C**IME DI RAPE, SOMETIMES CALLED **RAPINI**, AND MOST COMMONLY CALLED BROCCOLI RAAB IN AMERICA, IS A MEMBER OF THE TURNIP FAMILY; DESPITE THAT FACT, IT MORE CLOSELY RESEMBLES BROCCOLI IN APPEARANCE AND IN TASTE. THE VEGETABLE IS INTERCHANGEABLE WITH BROCCOLI IN THE CLASSIC **ORECCHIETTE CON SUGO DI RAPE** ("LITTLE EARS WITH **RAPE** SAUCE"), BUT **RAPE** HAS A UNIQUELY BITTER TASTE BELOVED BY THE ITALIANS. ACTUALLY, THE VEGETABLE IS MORE COMMONPLACE IN THE SOUTH OF ITALY THAN IN THE NORTH. IT BECAME PART OF MY MOTHER'S REPERTOIRE WHEN SHE CAME TO AMERICA, WHERE SHE LEARNED TO COOK IT FROM MY FATHER'S MOTHER, WHO HAD EMIGRATED FROM APULIA. ✿ AMERICAN COOKS HAVE A TENDENCY TO SAUTÉ THIS GREEN WITHOUT FIRST BOILING IT BECAUSE OF THE CURRENT AVERSION TO BOILING. THIS IS A MISTAKE, HOWEVER, FOR BOILING IT BRIEFLY BEFORE SAUTÉING RIDS IT OF EXCESSIVE BITTERNESS AND TENDERIZES THE STALKS.

*2 pounds* cime di rape

*1 tablespoon* salt

*3 tablespoons* extra-virgin olive oil

*1 large clove garlic, cut into small pieces*

*pinch of red pepper flakes, or to taste*

Using a small, sharp paring knife, peel off the skin from the tough lower stalks of the *rape* (most of the bottom portion of stalk). Cut the *rape* into approximately 3-inch lengths and wash it well. Fill a saucepan three-fourths full of water and bring to a rolling boil. Drain the *rape* and add it and the salt to the pan. Cover partially and cook for 5 minutes after the water returns to a boil.

Meanwhile, place the olive oil, garlic, and pepper flakes together in a cold skillet. Turn on the heat to low and sauté gently until the garlic starts to color (do not let it brown), about 5 minutes. Drain the *rape* and transfer it to the skillet (do not drain so thoroughly that the *rape* is dry; it should still be dripping somewhat when transferred to the skillet). Stir, cover, and cook gently, stirring occasionally, until tender, about 5 minutes longer.

Serve immediately.

# SCAROLA IN PADELLA

❋

SAUTÉED ESCAROLE

FOR 4 PEOPLE

**H**ERE IS A TYPICAL ITALIAN METHOD FOR COOKING GREENS, INCLUDING CURLY ENDIVE AND SPINACH. IF COOKING SPINACH IN THIS WAY, THE WATER SHOULD BE OMITTED, AND UNSALTED BUTTER CAN BE SUBSTITUTED FOR THE OLIVE OIL.

Remove any wilted outer leaves of the escarole. Cut off the tough bottom and trim off any brown spots. Cut the head crosswise into shreds 1 inch wide. Wash well to remove all dirt or sand

In a large skillet over low heat, warm the oil. Add the garlic and sauté until lightly golden, about 4 minutes. Add the escarole and the water. Cover and cook over medium heat until tender, about 15 minutes. Stir the contents occasionally to prevent the greens from sticking.

Add salt to taste, if desired. Serve immediately.

*1 large head escarole (about 2 pounds)*

*¼ cup extra-virgin olive oil*

*2 large cloves garlic, bruised*

*¼ cup water*

*salt (optional)*

# SPINACI CON AGLIO E LIMONE

✿

### SAUTÉED SPINACH WITH GARLIC AND LEMON ZEST

#### FOR 3 OR 4 PEOPLE

I HAVE BEEN PREPARING SPINACH THIS WAY FOR AS LONG AS I CAN REMEMBER. THE SPINACH HOLDS SOME OF ITS SHAPE, SO IT LOOKS STUNNING ON A SERVING PLATE COATED WITH THE BEGUILING COMBINATION OF LEMON ZEST, GARLIC, AND FRUITY OLIVE OIL. BECAUSE THE SPINACH IS TOSSED QUICKLY IN THE FRAGRANT OLIVE OIL OVER HIGH HEAT, IT WILTS BUT DOES NOT DISINTEGRATE THE WAY STEAMED OR BOILED SPINACH DOES. A BONUS OF THIS COOKING METHOD IS THAT ALL OF THE VITAMINS ARE RETAINED BECAUSE IT IS NOT COOKED LONG ENOUGH FOR THE WATER TO LEACH OUT OF THE LEAVES.

1-½ pounds spinach

3 tablespoons extra-virgin olive oil

3-inch-long strip lemon zest, blanched
    for 30 seconds, drained, and finely
    sliced crosswise

2 large cloves garlic, bruised

salt

freshly milled white pepper

Wash the spinach thoroughly in several changes of water to remove sand. Discard any yellow leaves; cut off and discard the stems. Drain but do not dry the spinach leaves.

Select a very large skillet that will accommodate all the spinach and allow you to toss it freely. Warm the oil in the skillet over medium heat. Add the lemon zest and garlic. Sauté until the garlic is colored but not browned, about 5 minutes. Increase the heat to medium-high. Add the spinach. As soon as it is all in the pan, toss it quickly with a wooden spoon. Coat the leaves with the hot oil until they wilt, but do not cook the spinach through. The leaves should not collapse into a mass from the heat; they should still retain their shape even though they will wilt.

Remove the skillet from the heat. Add salt and pepper to taste and serve.

# CAVOLO IN AGRODOLCE

❊

SAUTÉED SWEET-AND-SOUR CABBAGE WITH CARAWAY

FOR 6 PEOPLE

CABBAGE IS COOKED IN MANY STYLES IN ITALY. THE SIMPLEST IS PROBABLY THE SARDINIAN FASH-ION OF BOILING CABBAGE IN SALTED WATER UNTIL IT IS TENDER, AND THEN SPRINKLING IT WITH FRUITY OLIVE OIL (**CAULI A CONCA** IN SARDINIAN DIALECT). EVEN THIS ELEMENTARY DISH IS DELICIOUS IF THE CABBAGE IS YOUNG AND FRESH, AND THE IS OIL FULL-BODIED AND FLAVORFUL. ❊ THE FOLLOW-ING RECIPE IS ONE OF MY MOTHER'S WAYS OF COOKING CABBAGE AS A SIDE DISH. WITH ITS GERMANIC FLAVORS OF VINEGAR AND CARAWAY, IT IS REMININSCENT OF THE COOKING OF NORTHEASTERN ITALY.

Using a large, sharp knife, remove the hard core of the cabbage and then slice the head into fine shreds. You should have about 5 firmly packed cups.

In a Dutch oven over low heat, warm the vegetable oil. Add the onion and sauté gently until softened, about 5 minutes. Add the cabbage and stir to coat it with the oil. Add the caraway seeds, salt, sugar, and water. Cover and cook over low heat, stirring occasionally, until tender, about 15 minutes.

Remove the cover, add the vinegar, and cook until the vinegar evaporates, about 2 minutes longer. Serve hot.

*1 small head green cabbage*

*2 tablespoons vegetable oil*

*1 onion, quartered and thinly sliced*

*1 teaspoon caraway seeds*

*1 teaspoon salt*

*½ teaspoon sugar*

*¼ cup water*

*1 tablespoon red wine vinegar*

# PATATE SCHISCIONERA

❀

STEWED PARSLIED POTATOES, SARDINIA STYLE

FOR 6 PEOPLE

**M**Y MATERNAL GRANDMOTHER USED TO MAKE POTATOES THIS WAY. THE POTATOES ARE STEWED SLOWLY WITH GARLIC AND PARSLEY, WHICH MAKES THEM MOIST, CREAMY AND VERY FLAVORFUL. THIS IS A LOVELY SIDE DISH.

*2 tablespoons extra-virgin olive oil*

*2 large cloves garlic, finely chopped or grated*

*5 medium-sized boiling potatoes (about 1-½ pounds), peeled and cut into 1-inch cubes*

*1 cup water*

*½ teaspoon salt*

*freshly milled black pepper*

*2 tablespoons chopped fresh Italian parsley*

Place the oil and garlic in a cold saucepan large enough to accommodate the potatoes later. Turn on the heat to low and sauté until the garlic is softened, about 1 minute. Add the potatoes and stir. Add the water, salt, pepper to taste, and parsley. Cover and simmer over medium heat until potatoes are tender, about 15 minutes. Stir the potatoes occasionally as they cook to prevent them from sticking to the pan.

Serve immediately.

AHEAD-OF-TIME NOTE: This dish can be made up to 2 days in advance, then cooled, covered, and refrigerated. Reheat gently over low heat.

# INSALATA DI POMODORI

✱

## MARINATED TOMATO SALAD WITH OLIVES, CAPERS, AND HERBS

### FOR 4 PEOPLE

HERE IS A NICE WAY TO SERVE RAW TOMATOES IN SUMMER WHEN SWEET, VINE-RIPENED ONES CAN BE FOUND AT FARM STALLS OR IN HOME GARDENS. BECAUSE THERE IS NO VINEGAR IN THE DRESSING, THE TOMATOES RETAIN THEIR CRISPNESS WHILE THEY MARINATE IN THE GARLIC-INFUSED OLIVE OIL. THE SALAD CAN BE PREPARED IN A BOWL AS A GREEN SALAD WOULD BE, OR THE TOMATOES, AFTER BEING SEEDED, CAN BE SPREAD OUT ON A PLATTER AND SPRINKLED WITH THE CAPERS, OLIVES, HERBS, AND OLIVE OIL.

In a cup combine the oil and garlic. Using a spoon, push down on the cloves to release their juice into the oil. Set aside.

Cut the tomatoes in half lengthwise and remove the seeds, using your thumb to push them out. Slice the tomato halves into smaller wedges and place them in a salad bowl. Add the capers, olives, herbs, and pepper to taste; then add the oil and toss gently to mix. Add salt to taste.

Allow the salad to remain at room temperature for up to 1 hour before serving. Do not refrigerate or the flavor and texture will diminish.

2 tablespoons extra-virgin olive oil

2 cloves garlic, bruised

1-¼ pounds firm vine-ripened tomatoes

1 tablespoon drained small capers

¼ cup pitted and sliced, sharply flavored
   imported black olives

a small handful of fresh basil leaves
   (about 9), torn into small pieces

½ teaspoon fresh oregano leaves, or
   ¼ teaspoon dried oregano

freshly milled black pepper

salt

# INSALATA DI PANE ALLA PUGLIESE

✺

WHOLE-WHEAT BREAD AND TOMATO SALAD, APULIA STYLE

FOR 5 OR 6 PEOPLE

THE ITALIANS ARE VERY INVENTIVE WITH STALE BREAD. THEY USE IT AS A STARTING POINT FOR SALADS, SOUPS, BAKED DISHES, AND MANY OTHER THINGS. THIS BREAD SALAD IS NOT UNLIKE TUSCAN **PANZANELLA**, MADE WITH SALTLESS TUSCAN BREAD, OR THE APULIAN BREAD SALAD MADE WITH WHITE PEASANT BREAD CALLED **CIALEDD'** IN DIALECT. IT IS MADE FROM WHOLE-WHEAT BREAD, HOWEVER, WHICH GIVES IT A DIFFERENT TASTE AND TEXTURE FROM THOSE OTHER SALADS. THE AMOUNT OF WATER NEEDED WILL DEPEND UPON THE DRYNESS OF THE BREAD. THIS RECIPE IS BASED ON BREAD THAT IS SOME FOUR OR FIVE DAYS OLD — QUITE DRY, BUT NOT TOTALLY HARD. THE POINT IS TO ADD ENOUGH WATER TO THE SHREDDED BREAD TO MOISTEN IT WITHOUT MAKING IT SOGGY.

Slice the bread and tear it into approximately 1-inch pieces (it should yield about 3 cups). Put it in a salad bowl and sprinkle enough of the water over it to moisten it without making it soggy. Add the tomatoes, onion, and herbs.

In a separate small bowl, whisk together the olive oil and vinegar. Pour it over the bread salad. Add the salt and pepper and toss to mix well. Serve.

AHEAD-OF-TIME NOTE: This salad can be prepared up to 2 hours in advance of serving and kept at room temperature.

*½ pound stale whole-wheat bread, crusts removed (see recipe introduction)*

*½ cup water, or more depending upon dryness of bread*

*2 vine-ripened tomatoes, diced*

*½ red onion, quartered and finely sliced*

*2 tablespoons chopped fresh basil*

*1 teaspoon chopped fresh oregano, or ½ teaspon dried oregano*

*2 tablespoons chopped fresh Italian parsley*

*5 tablespoons extra-virgin olive oil*

*3 tablespoons red wine vinegar*

*¼ teaspoon salt, or to taste*

*⅛ teaspoon freshly milled black pepper, or to taste*

# INSALATA DI FAGIOLI

❈

BEAN SALAD

FOR 4 PEOPLE

THE TUSCANS, DUBBED **MANGIAFAGIOLI**, "BEAN EATERS," BY THEIR COUNTRYMEN, ARE PARTICU-LARLY FOND OF BEANS. THEIR SIMPLE BEAN DISHES REFLECT A RESTRAINED TEMPERAMENT AS ANCIENT AS THEIR ETRUSCAN ANCESTORS, AND ARE USUALLY BOUND TOGETHER BY THE AREA'S FAMED OLIVE OIL, WHICH IS THE REGION'S SOUL. THE SIMPLEST OF TUSCANY'S DELICIOUS REPERTOIRE OF BEAN DISHES IS ONE OF BOILED **CANNELLINI** BEANS ANOINTED WITH FRUITY EXTRA-VIRGIN OLIVE OIL. THIS **CONTORNO** IS SERVED WARM AND IF THE BEANS ARE FLAVORFUL AND THE OLIVE OIL IS GOOD, IT IS A REVELATION. BUT IN TUSCANY AS WELL AS OTHER REGIONS, BEANS AND LENTILS APPEAR IN SALADS SUCH AS THIS ONE, AS WELL AS IN HOT CONTORNI. ❈ BECAUSE OF THE SIMPLICITY OF THIS BEAN SALAD, THE ONLY OIL THAT IS APPROPRIATE IS THE HIGHEST-QUALITY EXTRA-VIRGIN OLIVE OIL.

1 cup dried cannellini beans or Great
    Northern beans (see page 15 to
    rehydrate and cook dried beans)

For the dressing:
¼ cup extra-virgin olive oil
2 tablespoons chopped sweet red or
    Vidalia onion
1 tablespoon chopped fresh Italian
    parsley
½ teaspoon chopped fresh marjoram,
    or ¼ teaspoon dried marjoram
2 tablespoons freshly squeezed lemon
    juice
1 teaspoon salt
¼ teaspoon freshly milled black pepper

Rehydrate and cook the beans as directed on page 15. Drain the beans well and place them in a serving bowl.

In a small bowl, whisk together all the ingredients for the dressing, mixing well. Toss the dressing with the beans and serve.

VARIATION: Add 1 cup cooked yellow wax beans, cooked al dente (tender but quite firm), to the salad, increasing the amount of dressing accordingly.

# MAIL-ORDER SOURCES

❊

## MAIL-ORDER SOURCES FOR ITALIAN COOKING EQUIPMENT AND PROVISIONS

AMERICAN SPOON FOODS
P.O. Box 566
Petoskey, Michigan 49770
616/347-9030, 800/222-5886
Dried morels, *porcini*, and *shiitakes*.

AUX DELICES DES BOIS, INC.
4 Leonard Street
New York, New York 10013
212/334-1230
All types of cultivated and imported mushrooms,
sun-dried tomatoes. Will accept phone orders
for overnight delivery.

DEAN & DELUCA
Mail-Order Department
560 Broadway
New York, New York 10012
212/431-1691, 800/221-7714, ext. 223 or 270
Kitchen equipment; Italian specialty foods,
imported dried mushrooms.
Catalog available.

G.B. RATTO INTERNATIONAL GROCER
821 Washington Street
Oakland, California 94607
800/228-3515 (California), 800/325-3483 (out of state)
Italian specialty foods, imported dried mushrooms,
large assortment of grains, flours, herbs, and spices.
Catalog available.

HANS JOHANSSON
44 West 74th Street
New York, New York 10023
212/787-6496
Dried morels, *porcini*, black trumpets,
*chanterelles*, and *shiitakes*.

MANGANARO FOODS
488 Ninth Avenue
New York, New York 10018
212/563-5331, 800/472-5264
Italian specialty foods, imported dried mushrooms.
Catalog available.

METRO AGRI BUSINESS
47 Wooster Street
New York, New York 10013
212/431-3504
Dried *porcini* and morels.

THE MOZZARELLA COMPANY
2944 Elm Street
Dallas, Texas 75226
214/741-4072, 800/798-2954
Large variety of fresh and aged cheeses;
sun-dried tomatoes; imported olive oils and balsamic
vinegar. Cheeses shipped overnight.

THE SANDY MUSH HERB NURSERY
Route 2, Surrett Cove Road
Leicester, North Carolina 28748
704/683-2014
Live herbs and herb seeds shipped.
Lovely illustrated catalog ($4, refundable with first order)
includes suggested herb-garden patterns, information
about growing and drying herbs, recipes.


SHEPHERD'S GARDEN SEEDS
Shipping Office
30 Irene Street
Torrington, Connecticut 06790
203/482-3638
Large selection of seeds for vegetables, herbs, and flowers.
Catalog available.


TODARO BROTHERS
555 Second Avenue
New York, New York 10016
212/679-7766
Italian specialty foods, imported cheeses.
Catalog available.


VIVANDE PORTA VIA
2125 Fillmore Street
San Francisco, California 94115
415/346-4430
Imported Italian seeds for hard-to-find Italian
vegetable varieties; Italian specialty foods.


WILLIAMS-SONOMA
Mail-Order Department
P.O. Box 7456
San Francisco, California 94120-7456
415/421-4242, 800/541-2233
Kitchen equipment; some Italian specialty foods.
Catalog available.


W. J. CLARK & CO.
5400 West Roosevelt Road
Chicago, Illinois 60650
312/626-3676, 800/229-0090
Dried *porcini*, *shiitakes*, morels, and oyster mushrooms;
chopped and powdered dried wild mushrooms.
Catalog available.


ZABAR'S
Mail-Order Department
2245 Broadway
New York, New York 10024
212/787-2003, 800/221-3347
Kitchen equipment; some Italian specialty
foods, imported cheeses.
Catalog available.

# INDEX

✵

# TABLE OF EQUIVALENTS

THE EXACT EQUIVALENTS IN THE FOLLOWING TABLES HAVE BEEN ROUNDED FOR CONVENIENCE.

### US/UK

oz=ounce
lb=pound
in=inch
ft=foot
tbl=tablespoon
fl oz=fluid ounce
qt=quart

### METRIC

g=gram
kg=kilogram
mm=millimeter
cm=centimeter
ml=milliliter
l=liter

### WEIGHTS

| US/UK | Metric |
|---|---|
| 1 oz | 30 g |
| 2 oz | 60 g |
| 3 oz | 90 g |
| 4 oz (¼ lb) | 125 g |
| 5 oz (⅓ lb) | 155 g |
| 6 oz | 185 g |
| 7 oz | 220 g |
| 8 oz (½ lb) | 250 g |
| 10 oz | 315 g |
| 12 oz (¾ lb) | 375 g |
| 14 oz | 440 g |
| 16 oz (1 lb) | 500 g |
| 1½ lb | 750 g |
| 2 lb | 1 kg |
| 3 lb | 1.5 kg |

### OVEN TEMPERATURES

| Fahrenheit | Celsius | Gas |
|---|---|---|
| 250 | 20 | ½ |
| 275 | 140 | 1 |
| 300 | 150 | 2 |
| 325 | 160 | 3 |
| 350 | 180 | 4 |
| 375 | 190 | 5 |
| 400 | 200 | 6 |
| 425 | 220 | 7 |
| 450 | 230 | 8 |
| 475 | 240 | 9 |
| 500 | 260 | 10 |

### LIQUIDS

| US | Metric | UK |
|---|---|---|
| 2 tbl | 30 ml | 1 fl oz |
| ¼ cup | 60 ml | 2 fl oz |
| ⅓ cup | 80 ml | 3 fl oz |
| ½ cup | 125 ml | 4 fl oz |
| ⅔ cup | 160 ml | 5 fl oz |
| ¾ cup | 180 ml | 6 fl oz |
| 1 cup | 250 ml | 8 fl oz |
| 1½ cups | 75 ml | 12 fl oz |
| 2 cups | 500 ml | 16 fl oz |
| 4 cups/1 qt | 1 l | 32 fl oz |

### LENGTH MEASURES

| | |
|---|---|
| ⅛ in | 3 mm |
| ¼ in | 6 mm |
| ½ in | 12 mm |
| 1 in | 2.5 cm |
| 2 in | 5 cm |
| 3 in | 7.5 cm |
| 4 in | 10 cm |
| 5 in | 13 cm |
| 6 in | 15 cm |
| 7 in | 18 cm |
| 8 in | 20 cm |
| 9 in | 23 cm |
| 10 in | 25 cm |
| 11 in | 28 cm |
| 12/1 ft | 30 cm |

### All-purpose (plain) flour / dried bread crumbs / chopped nuts

| | | |
|---|---|---|
| ¼ cup | I oz | 30 g |
| ⅓ cup | 1½ oz | 45 g |
| ½ cup | 2 oz | 60 g |
| ¾ cup | 3 oz | 90 g |
| I cup | 4 oz | 125 g |
| 1½ cups | 6 oz | 185 g |
| 2 cups | 8 oz | 250 g |

### Whole-Wheat (Wholemeal) Flour

| | | |
|---|---|---|
| 3 tbl | I oz | 30 g |
| ½ cup | 2 oz | 60 g |
| ⅔ cup | 3 oz | 90 g |
| I cup | 4 oz | 125 g |
| 1¼ cups | 5 oz | 155 g |
| 1⅔ cups | 7 oz | 210 g |
| 1¾ cups | 8 oz | 250 g |

### Brown Sugar

| | | |
|---|---|---|
| ¼ cup | 1½ oz | 45 g |
| ½ cup | 3 oz | 90 g |
| ¾ cup | 4 oz | 125 g |
| I cup | 5½ oz | 170 g |
| 1½ cups | 8 oz | 250 g |
| 2 cups | 10 oz | 315 g |

### White Sugar

| | | |
|---|---|---|
| ¼ cup | 2 oz | 60 g |
| ⅓ cup | 3 oz | 90 g |
| ½ cup | 4 oz | 125 g |
| ¾ cup | 6 oz | 185 g |
| I cup | 8 oz | 250 g |
| 1½ cups | 12 oz | 375 g |
| 2 cups | I lb | 500 g |

### Raisins / Currants / Semolina

| | | |
|---|---|---|
| ¼ cup | I oz | 30 g |
| ⅓ cup | 2 oz | 60 g |
| ½ cup | 3 oz | 90 g |
| ¾ cup | 4 oz | 125 g |
| I cup | 5 oz | 155 g |

### Long-Grain Rice / Cornmeal

| | | |
|---|---|---|
| ⅓ cup | 2 oz | 60 g |
| ½ cup | 2½ oz | 75 g |
| ¾ cup | 4 oz | 125 g |
| I cup | 5 oz | 155 g |
| 1½ cups | 8 oz | 250 g |

### Dried Beans

| | | |
|---|---|---|
| ¼ cup | 1½ oz | 45 g |
| ⅓ cup | 2 oz | 60 g |
| ½ cup | 3 oz | 90 g |
| ¾ cup | 5 oz | 155 g |
| I cup | 6 oz | 185 g |
| 1¼ cups | 8 oz | 250 g |
| 1½ cups | 12 oz | 375 g |

### Rolled Oats

| | | |
|---|---|---|
| ⅓ cup | I oz | 30 g |
| ⅔ cup | 2 oz | 60 g |
| I cup | 3 oz | 90 g |
| 1½ cups | 4 oz | 125 g |
| 2 cups | 5 oz | 155 g |

### Jam / Honey

| | | |
|---|---|---|
| 2 tbl | 2 oz | 60 g |
| ¼ cup | 3 oz | 90 g |
| ½ cup | 5 oz | 155 g |
| ¾ cup | 8 oz | 250 g |
| I cup | II oz | 345 g |

### Grated Parmesan / Romano Cheese

| | | |
|---|---|---|
| ¼ cup | I oz | 30 g |
| ½ cup | 2 oz | 60 g |
| ¾ cup | 3 oz | 90 g |
| I cup | 4 oz | 125 g |
| 1⅓ cups | 5 oz | 155 g |
| 2 cups | 7 oz | 220 g |